THE PROBLEM
ΙS YOU!

101 PROBLEMS THAT KEEP *YOU* FROM YOUR
BEST LIFE AND HOW *YOU* CAN SOLVE THEM

ALLEN BROWN

BUILD OUR KINGDOM PUBLISHING
—— BUILD OUR KINGDOM.COM ——

The Problem Is You!

Printed in the United States of America

1st Edition December 2024 First Printing

ISBN paperback: 978-1-964203-06-5

Build Our Kingdom Publishing, LLC. 560 Main St, Stroudsburg, PA 18360

www.BuildOurKingdom.com

Edited by: Allen Brown, ChatGPT

Scripture taken from the New King James Version®. Copyright © 1982 by Thomas Nelson. Used by permission. All rights reserved.

Scripture quotations marked (NIV) are taken from the Holy Bible, New International Version®, NIV®. Copyright © 1973, 19 78, 1984, 2011 by Biblica, Inc.™ Used by permission of Zondervan. All rights reserved worldwide. www.zondervan.com The "NIV" and "New International Version" are trademarks registered in the United States Patent and Trademark Office by Biblica, Inc™

Table of Contents

EDUCATION PROBLEMS

TIME MANAGEMENT PROBLEMS

LEADERSHIP PROBLEMS

SELF-WORTH PROBLEMS

INTRODUCTION

Life is full of challenges that can hold you back from reaching your potential. From struggles in relationships and career to obstacles in business and personal growth, there are numerous factors that can stop you from progressing, and often, you don't even realize they're in your way. The reason I wrote this book is to bring awareness to these hidden influences. It's not meant to blame you for your circumstances but to encourage self-reflection so you can move past the things that are limiting you.

While the title of this book may sound harsh—"The Problem Is You"—the intention is not to point a finger or assign guilt. It's to open your eyes to the subconscious patterns that might be holding you back in areas like career, relationships, and business. These patterns often operate beneath the surface, guiding your decisions without you even realizing it. The truth is, once you recognize these patterns, you can change them and create the life you truly desire.

In my previous book, *Your Life Is Not a Coincidence*, I introduced a three-pillar framework to understanding the forces that shape our lives.

THESE PILLARS ARE:

1. **God's Divine Hand** – The higher power guiding and orchestrating the events of your life.
2. **Conscious Decisions** – The choices you make, intentionally or not, that set the course for your future.
3. **Subconscious Influences** – The hidden forces operating within you that shape your decisions without your awareness.

1

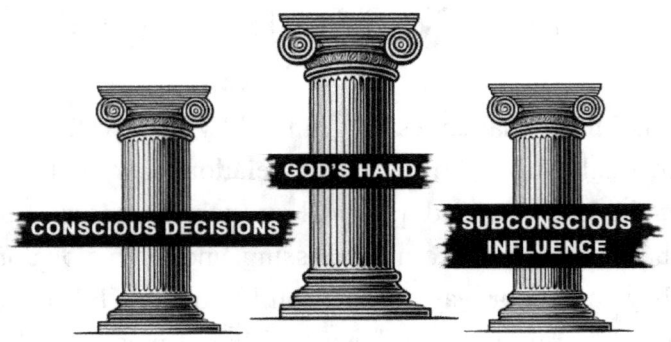

While the first book explored all three pillars, this one will focus exclusively on the third: **Subconscious Influences**. This is the most subtle, yet powerful pillar, and often the one that holds us back the most. It's the part of you that shapes your thoughts, behaviors, and outcomes, even when you're not conscious of it. This book is designed to help you recognize and address these subconscious forces so you can break free from the cycles that keep you stuck.

You might be wondering, "Why focus on me?" The truth is, it's difficult to face the fact that many of the struggles we face come from within. It's easier to blame external circumstances, other people, or bad luck. But once you realize that the root of the problem often lies in your own subconscious influences, you can take responsibility and, more importantly, take action to change. And that is the liberating part—the solution is within you.

In the chapters ahead, we'll dive into the eight elements of subconscious influence: **Beliefs**, **Habits**, **Fears**, **Biases**, **Memories**, **Assumptions**, **Motivations**, and **Expectations**. Each chapter will be structured in a way that not only brings awareness to these subconscious elements but also gives you a real-life scenario to illustrate how these hidden forces operate in your life.

Here's how each chapter is broken down for your understanding:

REAL-LIFE SCENARIO

For example, let's say you're struggling with money. One problem might be **Believing Debt Is Inevitable**—something that many of us subconsciously take for granted. In this section, I will share a story about someone facing this issue. You will see how their subconscious influences, such as **Beliefs, Fears**, and **Memories**, have shaped their financial mindset and decisions. These specific subconscious influences will be highlighted in **bold** so you can easily identify which parts of the subconscious are contributing to the problem.

1. SUBCONSCIOUS INFLUENCES

After the scenario, I will dive deeper into the subconscious influences affecting the person in the story. This section helps you understand how these elements—like **Fears, Assumptions**, or **Motivations**—are silently shaping their actions and outcomes.

2. ROOT CAUSE

Next, we break down the root cause of the problem, helping you understand why this belief or habit has taken root in your life. You'll gain clarity on how certain patterns or beliefs have been passed down or formed, and how they continue to affect your decisions.

3. YOUR SOLUTION

Following the exploration of the root cause, you'll find **Your Solution** section, which offers actionable strategies to break free from the subconscious influences that are keeping you stuck. This part is designed to give you practical tools for change.

4. SCRIPTURE REFERENCE

To ground the solution in biblically sound advice, we'll include a **Scripture Reference**. Each solution will align with a biblical principle, providing wisdom and guidance to help you make lasting changes.

5. CLOSING THOUGHT

Finally, each problem concludes with a **Closing Thought**. This section encourages you to reflect on what you've learned and apply the solution to your own life. It's designed to give you a moment of introspection, helping you internalize the solution and begin the process of change.

The goal of this structure is to give you a clear understanding of how subconscious influences shape your life and provide practical solutions for overcoming them. This is not a book to make you feel guilty; it's a tool for you to reflect on how you may be holding yourself back, so you can break free from old patterns and take control of your future.

Together, let's uncover the subconscious influences that have been hindering your success and move toward a new path of intentionality, growth, and freedom.

MONEY PROBLEMS

Problem 1: Believing Debt Is Inevitable

**How your mindset about debt keeps
you trapped in financial struggles.**

Have you ever told yourself, "Debt is just a part of life"? Many people operate with the subconscious belief that living with debt is normal and unavoidable. This mindset silently sabotages your financial health, keeping you stuck in a cycle of borrowing and repayment without ever achieving true freedom. What if the real problem isn't the debt itself but the way you think about it?

SUBCONSCIOUS INFLUENCES

Imagine a young professional, Jason, who graduated with student loans and immediately leased a car, believing it was the next logical step. As his life progressed, Jason relied on credit cards to bridge gaps in his monthly budget, rationalizing that he'd pay everything off once he earned more. But as his income grew, so did his expenses, leaving him in an endless cycle of borrowing and repayment. Jason's belief that debt is unavoidable wasn't just circumstantial; it was deeply rooted in subconscious influences.

From an early age, Jason absorbed messages that shaped his financial perspective. He grew up hearing that "everyone has debt," shaping his view through *beliefs* that borrowing is a necessary part of adulthood. Overspending became a *habit*, with credit cards offering a convenient safety net. His *fear* of missing out on life's pleasures pushed him to spend beyond his means, while cultural *biases* reinforced the idea that borrowing was a valid way to achieve the lifestyle he desired. Jason's *memories* of his parents' financial struggles led to an *assumption* that living paycheck to paycheck was normal. Motivated by instant gratification and anchored by *expectations* that debt is manageable, Jason never questioned whether a debt-free life was achievable.

ROOT CAUSE

Debt feels inevitable because it's deeply ingrained in how you perceive finances. From societal norms to personal experiences, the idea of debt as a necessary tool prevents you from considering alternatives. This mindset keeps you from seeking freedom and prioritizing financial discipline.

YOUR SOLUTION
1. **Challenge Your Beliefs:** Reflect on whether debt is truly necessary or just convenient.
2. **Set a Debt-Free Vision:** Imagine your life without debt—less stress, more options, and greater freedom.
3. **Delay Gratification:** Avoid using credit for non-essentials and save for what you need.
4. **Create a Budget:** Take control by tracking your spending and focusing on debt elimination.
5. **Celebrate Progress:** Recognize small victories as you pay down debt to stay motivated.

SCRIPTURE REFERENCE

"The rich rule over the poor, and the borrower is slave to the lender." (Proverbs 22:7)

This verse reminds you that debt creates dependency, and freedom comes from living within your means.

CLOSING THOUGHT

Debt may feel inevitable, but it's a mindset you can change. By challenging the subconscious influences keeping you stuck, you can take steps toward financial freedom. Where is debt holding you back, and what will you do today to break free? The choice is yours.

Problem 2: Fearing Wealth Will Change You

**How your fear of success keeps you from
reaching financial abundance.**

Have you ever hesitated to pursue greater financial success because you're afraid it might change who you are? Many people subconsciously fear that accumulating wealth will lead them to become greedy, arrogant, or disconnected from their values. This fear can act as a barrier, preventing you from achieving your full financial potential. But what if the real issue isn't wealth itself, but your perception of how it might transform you?

SUBCONSCIOUS INFLUENCES

Consider Alex, who grew up in a community where wealth was often associated with negative traits. His **beliefs** were shaped by hearing phrases like "money changes people," leading him to associate financial success with moral compromise. These **memories** created a **bias** against pursuing wealth, as he feared it would distance him from his roots. Alex's **fears** of being judged by friends and family for seeking financial abundance further reinforced his reluctance. His **assumptions** that wealth leads to corruption and his **expectations** of losing personal integrity if he becomes wealthy keep him from striving for financial growth. These subconscious influences trap Alex in a cycle of self-sabotage, preventing him from achieving his financial aspirations.

ROOT CAUSE

The fear that wealth will change you often stems from societal narratives and personal experiences that portray financial success as inherently corrupting. These deep-seated beliefs can lead to self-imposed limitations, causing you to avoid opportunities for financial growth to maintain your perceived moral integrity.

YOUR SOLUTION

1. **Reframe Your Beliefs:** Understand that wealth is a tool that reflects the character of its holder. It can be used for positive purposes when aligned with your values.
2. **Identify Negative Associations:** Reflect on past experiences and societal messages that have shaped your view of wealth. Challenge whether these associations are universally true.
3. **Align Wealth With Values:** Consider how financial success can enable you to make a positive impact, such as supporting charitable causes or providing for loved ones.
4. **Seek Positive Role Models:** Surround yourself with individuals who have achieved financial success while maintaining their integrity and contributing positively to society.
5. **Practice Self-Compassion:** Recognize that aspiring for financial abundance doesn't make you a bad person. It's possible to be both wealthy and virtuous.

SCRIPTURE REFERENCE

"Command those who are rich in this present world not to be arrogant nor to put their hope in wealth, which is so uncertain, but to put their hope in God, who richly provides us with everything for our enjoyment." (1 Timothy 6:17) This verse reminds you that wealth itself isn't the problem; it's how you view and use it that determines its impact on your life and character.

CLOSING THOUGHT

Fearing that wealth will change you can hinder your financial growth and personal development. By examining and reshaping your subconscious beliefs, you can pursue financial success without compromising your values. Reflect on how your perceptions of wealth affect your financial decisions and consider steps to align your pursuit of success with your core beliefs

Problem 3: Trading Time for Dollars

How focusing only on earned income
limits your financial growth.

Do you believe working harder or longer hours is the key to wealth? Many people grow up with the mindset that exchanging time for money is the only way to achieve financial success. While this approach can provide stability, it often creates a ceiling on what you can earn. The problem isn't hard work itself—it's failing to recognize how to make money work for you.

SUBCONSCIOUS INFLUENCES

Take Lisa, a dedicated teacher who works tirelessly to provide for her family. Her *beliefs* about money, shaped by her upbringing, tell her that success comes only from relentless effort. These *memories* of her parents working multiple jobs instilled a *bias* against pursuing passive income, which feels unfamiliar and risky. Lisa's *fear* of failure keeps her from exploring options like investing or entrepreneurship.

Lisa assumes she must trade time for dollars because that's what she's always known. Her *motivations* to provide for her family drive her to work harder, not smarter, while her *expectations* for financial freedom remain tied to the hope of a future raise or promotion. These subconscious influences prevent Lisa from stepping into opportunities that could generate wealth without relying solely on her time.

ROOT CAUSE

The root of this problem lies in a lack of financial education and an overreliance on earned income. Society often promotes hard work as the ultimate path to success, but this mindset neglects the potential of leveraging assets like real estate, investments, or businesses. By focusing only on earning money through labor, you limit your capacity for wealth creation.

YOUR SOLUTION

1. **Shift Your Mindset:** Recognize that wealth comes from leveraging money, not just working harder.
2. **Educate Yourself:** Learn about investments, real estate, or other passive income streams that align with your goals.
3. **Start Small:** Take your first step by exploring low-risk opportunities, such as high-yield savings or simple investments.
4. **Build Assets:** Invest in things like property, businesses, or intellectual property that can generate income without requiring constant effort.
5. **Plan for Growth:** Set long-term financial goals that prioritize asset-building over hourly wages.

SCRIPTURE REFERENCE

"Invest in seven ventures, yes, in eight; you do not know what disaster may come upon the land." (Ecclesiastes 11:2)
This verse encourages diversification and planning, reminding you of the importance of creating multiple streams of income.

CLOSING THOUGHT

Relying solely on trading time for money keeps you in a cycle of financial limitation. By shifting your focus to building assets and leveraging resources, you can create wealth that works for you. What steps will you take today to start building the foundation for financial freedom? Remember, true wealth comes from strategy, not just effort.

Problem 4: Expecting Wealth Without Discipline

How a lack of financial self-control
keeps you from achieving success.

Do you find yourself dreaming of wealth but struggling to manage the money you already have? Many people have big financial goals yet fail to establish the discipline needed to achieve them. Without clear boundaries and intentional planning, even the best financial opportunities can slip away. The problem isn't your ambition—it's your lack of structure.

SUBCONSCIOUS INFLUENCES

Consider Daniel, who earns a steady income but often finds himself living paycheck to paycheck. His *beliefs* that financial discipline requires sacrificing happiness keep him from creating a budget. Past *memories* of his parents spending impulsively taught him that money is meant to be enjoyed, not restricted. This creates a *bias* that prioritizes instant gratification over long-term stability.

Daniel's *habits* include spending without tracking expenses, and his *fears* of missing out on life's pleasures drive impulsive purchases. He *assumes* that as long as he earns enough, managing money isn't necessary, and his *expectations* that wealth will eventually come through luck or promotions keep him from taking proactive steps. These subconscious patterns block Daniel from building the financial foundation required for success.

ROOT CAUSE

The root of this problem lies in the belief that wealth can be achieved without discipline. Financial success requires consistent planning, accountability, and the ability to delay gratification.

Without these, your resources can quickly deplete, no matter how much money you earn.

YOUR SOLUTION

1. **Create a Budget:** Develop a simple, realistic plan for managing your income and expenses.
2. **Track Your Spending:** Monitor where your money goes to identify areas where you can cut back.
3. **Set Financial Goals:** Establish clear, actionable objectives, such as saving for investments or reducing debt.
4. **Practice Delayed Gratification:** Postpone unnecessary purchases to focus on long-term rewards.
5. **Automate Savings:** Set up automatic transfers to ensure you consistently save and invest.

SCRIPTURE REFERENCE

"Whoever gathers money little by little makes it grow."
(Proverbs 13:11)
This verse emphasizes the importance of steady, disciplined effort in building lasting wealth.

CLOSING THOUGHT

Dreaming of wealth without practicing discipline is like planting seeds but never watering them. True financial success begins with small, intentional actions that build over time. Reflect on your spending habits and consider what changes you can make today to align your financial behavior with your long-term goals. Wealth doesn't come by chance—it comes through preparation.

Problem 5: Avoiding Financial Responsibility

**How ignoring accountability keeps you
from achieving financial freedom.**

Do you find it easier to blame external circumstances for your financial struggles rather than take ownership of them? Many people unknowingly sabotage their progress by avoiding financial responsibility. The issue isn't always a lack of resources—it's often the unwillingness to take control of what you already have. Without accountability, financial success remains out of reach.

SUBCONSCIOUS INFLUENCES

Think about Mia, who constantly struggles with her finances despite earning a decent salary. Her **beliefs** tell her that life is unpredictable, so there's no point in planning for the future. Childhood **memories** of her parents arguing over money created a **bias** that financial conversations are stressful and should be avoided. Mia's **fear** of confronting her spending habits prevents her from looking at her bank statements or setting a budget.

Her **habits** include ignoring bills until they're overdue, and she **assumes** that something external, like a raise or a windfall, will solve her problems. Her **motivations** are rooted in maintaining a comfortable lifestyle, even if it means accruing debt, and her **expectations** that someone else will help her out in the future keep her from taking full control. These influences keep Mia in a cycle of avoidance, with no clear path to financial freedom.

ROOT CAUSE

The root of this problem is a lack of financial ownership. When you avoid responsibility, you give away your power to improve your circumstances. True financial freedom requires acknowledging your role in your current situation and taking consistent, intentional steps toward change.

YOUR SOLUTION

1. **Own Your Situation:** Reflect on your finances honestly and take responsibility for where you are.
2. **Track Income and Expenses:** Create a detailed picture of your financial situation to identify problem areas.
3. **Address Debts:** Make a realistic plan to tackle overdue bills or loans.
4. **Set Boundaries:** Limit unnecessary spending and avoid financial commitments you can't manage.
5. **Seek Guidance:** Work with a financial advisor or use budgeting tools to stay accountable.

SCRIPTURE REFERENCE

"The plans of the diligent lead to profit as surely as haste leads to poverty." (Proverbs 21:5)
This verse reminds you that success comes from thoughtful planning and diligence, not avoidance.

CLOSING THOUGHT

Avoiding financial responsibility only delays the freedom you desire. By taking ownership of your finances, you can regain control and build a future aligned with your goals. What steps can you take today to stop avoiding and start owning your financial journey? The sooner you start, the sooner you'll see results.

CAREER PROBLEMS

Problem 6: Fearing Success Will Bring More Pressure

How avoiding growth limits your potential for achievement.

Do you find yourself hesitant to push for success because of what it might demand from you? Many people fear that achieving their goals will lead to overwhelming expectations, greater scrutiny, or even failure in the next phase. This fear keeps you from embracing opportunities that could elevate your life. The problem isn't success—it's your anxiety about what comes with it.

SUBCONSCIOUS INFLUENCES

Imagine Lisa, who's been offered a promotion at work but hesitates to accept it. Her *beliefs* that greater success will lead to more stress and less time for herself hold her back. Past *memories* of watching others struggle with high-pressure roles reinforce a *bias* against seeking advancement. Lisa's *fear* of not meeting expectations drives her to stay where she feels safe, even if it means giving up growth opportunities.

Lisa *assumes* that more responsibility will lead to inevitable burnout, and her *expectations* that success will bring unhappiness keep her from exploring what she's truly capable of. Motivated by the desire to maintain balance, Lisa avoids pursuing her full potential, leaving her unfulfilled and stagnant.

ROOT CAUSE

The root of this problem lies in associating success with negative consequences rather than opportunities. Fear of increased

15

demands and scrutiny often stems from a lack of confidence in your ability to adapt and thrive under new circumstances.

YOUR SOLUTION

1. **Redefine Success:** Understand that success can be a positive force for growth and fulfillment.
2. **Focus on Preparation:** Build the skills and systems needed to handle greater responsibility.
3. **Embrace Adaptability:** Recognize that challenges can be managed with time, effort, and support.
4. **Seek Role Models:** Learn from people who balance success with happiness and personal growth.
5. **Take Small Steps:** Pursue success incrementally to build confidence and reduce overwhelm.

SCRIPTURE REFERENCE

"For the Spirit God gave us does not make us timid, but gives us power, love, and self-discipline." (2 Timothy 1:7) This verse encourages you to approach new challenges with courage and confidence, knowing that you are equipped to succeed.

CLOSING THOUGHT

Fearing that success will bring more pressure can prevent you from reaching your true potential. By addressing the subconscious beliefs fueling this fear, you can embrace growth with confidence and excitement. What opportunity are you holding back from because of fear? Take one step today to move toward it, trusting that you have the strength to handle what comes next.

Problem 7: Assuming Hard Work Speaks for Itself

How relying solely on effort limits your career growth.

Do you believe that hard work alone is enough to get ahead? Many people assume that dedication and effort will naturally lead to recognition and success. While hard work is essential, failing to communicate your contributions or strategically align them with your goals can leave you overlooked and undervalued. The problem isn't your work ethic—it's assuming it's all you need.

SUBCONSCIOUS INFLUENCES

Take Kevin, a diligent employee who works late every night but never speaks up about his accomplishments. His *beliefs* that humility is a virtue keep him from advocating for himself. Past *memories* of being praised for effort alone reinforce a *bias* that results will always follow hard work. Kevin's *fear* of being seen as boastful prevents him from highlighting his achievements to leadership.

He *assumes* his dedication is obvious to others, even though no one truly notices the extent of his contributions. Motivated by the desire to be seen as a team player, Kevin avoids self-promotion. His *expectations* that promotions and opportunities will come automatically keep him stuck in the same position, frustrated and underappreciated.

ROOT CAUSE

The root of this problem lies in the belief that effort alone guarantees success. Without visibility, recognition, and alignment with strategic goals, even the hardest work can go unnoticed. Success requires both action and communication.

YOUR SOLUTION

1. **Track Your Contributions:** Keep a record of your accomplishments to build confidence and clarity.
2. **Communicate Strategically:** Share your successes in a way that highlights your value without appearing boastful.
3. **Seek Feedback:** Regularly ask for input to ensure your efforts align with organizational or personal goals.
4. **Align Efforts With Impact:** Focus your hard work on areas that directly contribute to measurable results.
5. **Build Relationships:** Cultivate connections with mentors or leaders who can advocate for you.

SCRIPTURE REFERENCE

"Whatever you do, work at it with all your heart, as working for the Lord, not for human masters." (Colossians 3:23) This verse reminds you to work with purpose and integrity, but also to ensure your efforts serve a meaningful purpose.

CLOSING THOUGHT

Assuming hard work speaks for itself can leave your contributions unnoticed and undervalued. By learning to strategically communicate your efforts, you can align your actions with your goals and create opportunities for growth. What step can you take today to ensure your hard work gets the recognition it deserves? Remember, effort paired with intention leads to success.

Problem 8: Believing You're Not Qualified Enough

How self-doubt prevents you from pursuing career opportunities.

Do you ever hesitate to apply for a position or take on a project because you don't think you're qualified? Many people let self-doubt stop them from advancing, assuming they need more experience or skills before they can succeed. This mindset often prevents you from recognizing your potential and taking steps toward your goals. The problem isn't your qualifications—it's your belief in your ability to grow into them.

SUBCONSCIOUS INFLUENCES

Consider Maya, a talented graphic designer who constantly undervalues her work. Her **beliefs** that she needs to master every skill before she's ready for a promotion keep her stuck in her current role. Past **memories** of being told she wasn't "good enough" in school reinforce a **bias** toward underestimating herself.

Maya's **fear** of rejection leads her to avoid applying for challenging positions, while her **assumptions** that others are always more qualified discourage her from trying. Motivated by perfectionism, she delays progress, and her **expectations** that success should come only after years of effort prevent her from seizing opportunities. These subconscious influences keep her from stepping into her full potential.

ROOT CAUSE

The root of this problem lies in a fixed mindset that equates qualifications with perfection. Growth requires taking risks and learning through experience, not waiting until you feel 100% ready.

Focusing on what you lack instead of what you offer limits your career trajectory.

YOUR SOLUTION

1. **Challenge Self-Doubt:** Recognize that no one is ever fully prepared for a new role—growth happens on the job.
2. **Focus on Strengths:** Highlight your unique skills and how they add value to the opportunity.
3. **Take Small Steps:** Apply for roles or projects slightly outside your comfort zone to build confidence.
4. **Seek Mentorship:** Surround yourself with mentors who can help you see your potential and encourage you to act.
5. **Reframe Rejection:** View setbacks as part of the journey, not as proof of inadequacy.

SCRIPTURE REFERENCE

"God does not call the qualified; He qualifies the called."
(Paraphrased from 2 Corinthians 3:5-6)

This principle reminds you that your abilities grow as you step into opportunities, not before.

CLOSING THOUGHT

Believing you're not qualified enough holds you back from the growth you're capable of achieving. By shifting your focus to your strengths and potential, you can overcome self-doubt and take the steps needed to move forward. What opportunity are you hesitating to pursue, and how can you act on it today? Remember, readiness is built through action, not waiting.

Problem 9: Avoiding Risk to Stay Comfortable

How fear of failure limits your career growth.

Do you hesitate to step outside your comfort zone, even when it could lead to greater opportunities? Many people avoid risk in their careers, prioritizing safety and predictability over the possibility of growth. While this mindset may feel secure, it often limits your ability to achieve success. The problem isn't the risks—it's your reluctance to embrace them.

SUBCONSCIOUS INFLUENCES

Take Eric, a software developer who has been in the same role for years, even though he dreams of leading a team. His **beliefs** that risk leads to failure stem from his past experiences of trying and falling short. These **memories** reinforce a **bias** toward avoiding challenges that could result in disappointment.

Eric's **fear** of failure keeps him from applying for leadership roles, while his **assumptions** that others are more capable prevent him from taking initiative. Motivated by the desire for stability, he remains in his comfort zone, and his **expectations** that risk will always lead to negative outcomes hold him back from pursuing meaningful opportunities. These subconscious influences keep Eric from reaching his full potential.

ROOT CAUSE

The root of this problem lies in an overemphasis on safety and an underestimation of your ability to adapt. Risk is an inherent part of growth, and avoiding it often means missing out on opportunities to learn, achieve, and excel in your career.

YOUR SOLUTION

1. **Reframe Risk:** Understand that failure is a natural part of growth and can lead to valuable lessons.
2. **Take Calculated Risks:** Start small by stepping into opportunities that challenge you without overwhelming you.
3. **Build Resilience:** Reflect on past challenges you've overcome to strengthen your confidence in handling setbacks.
4. **Seek Support:** Surround yourself with mentors or colleagues who encourage and guide you through risk-taking.
5. **Focus on the Bigger Picture:** Align your risks with long-term goals to keep your perspective grounded in growth.

SCRIPTURE REFERENCE

"Be strong and courageous. Do not be afraid; do not be discouraged, for the Lord your God will be with you wherever you go." (Joshua 1:9)
This verse reminds you to trust in your strength and step forward with faith, even when facing uncertainty.

CLOSING THOUGHT

Avoiding risk to stay comfortable may feel safe, but it often comes at the cost of your potential. By embracing calculated risks, you open doors to greater achievements and personal growth. What step can you take today to move beyond your comfort zone? Remember, progress begins where comfort ends.

BUSINESS PROBLEMS

Problem 10: Underestimating the Power of Networking

How neglecting connections hinders your career advancement.

Do you focus solely on your skills and experience, assuming they're all you need to succeed? Many people underestimate the importance of building and maintaining professional relationships, relying instead on hard work alone to open doors. The problem isn't your abilities—it's your failure to leverage the power of networking.

SUBCONSCIOUS INFLUENCES

Think of Alex, a highly capable engineer who struggles to get noticed for promotions. His **beliefs** that success should come from merit alone make him reluctant to network. Past **memories** of seeing others succeed through connections rather than skill reinforce a **bias** against networking as unfair.

Alex's **fear** of rejection or seeming opportunistic prevents him from reaching out, while his **assumptions** that others won't find value in him keep him isolated. Motivated by the desire to appear self-reliant, Alex avoids building relationships, and his **expectations** that success will happen organically without networking leave him stagnant. These subconscious patterns limit his opportunities for growth and advancement.

ROOT CAUSE

The root of this problem lies in a misunderstanding of networking as superficial or manipulative. True networking is about mutual support, collaboration, and creating opportunities for both parties. Neglecting it leaves you disconnected from valuable resources and insights.

YOUR SOLUTION

1. **Redefine Networking:** View it as building meaningful, mutually beneficial relationships rather than self-promotion.
2. **Start Small:** Attend events or connect with colleagues in low-pressure settings to ease into networking.
3. **Be Genuine:** Focus on offering value and support to others rather than solely seeking help for yourself.
4. **Leverage Existing Connections:** Reconnect with old colleagues or mentors who can provide guidance or opportunities.
5. **Set Networking Goals:** Aim to make a certain number of new connections each month to stay proactive.

SCRIPTURE REFERENCE

"Let us consider how we may spur one another on toward love and good deeds." (Hebrews 10:24)
This verse highlights the importance of supporting and encouraging one another, reflecting the essence of true networking.

CLOSING THOUGHT

Underestimating the power of networking limits your potential to grow and succeed. By embracing relationships as opportunities for collaboration and mutual benefit, you can unlock doors that hard work alone may not open. Who can you connect with today to take a step toward building a stronger professional network? Remember, success often comes through the people you surround yourself with.

Problem 11: Fearing Delegation Will Lead to Failure

How holding on too tightly limits your business growth.

Do you resist delegating tasks because you think no one else will do them as well as you? Many leaders and entrepreneurs fear that letting go of control will result in mistakes, inefficiency, or failure. This mindset often leads to burnout, missed opportunities, and a bottleneck in your business. The problem isn't delegation—it's your reluctance to trust others.

SUBCONSCIOUS INFLUENCES

Consider Maria, a business owner who insists on managing every detail of her operations. Her **beliefs** that "if you want something done right, do it yourself" keep her from sharing responsibilities. Past **memories** of employees failing to meet her standards reinforce a **bias** against trusting others.

Maria's **fear** of mistakes and **assumptions** that others can't handle critical tasks make her reluctant to delegate. Motivated by the desire to maintain control, she **expects** that her direct involvement is the only way to ensure success. These subconscious influences leave Maria overwhelmed and prevent her business from scaling.

ROOT CAUSE

The root of this problem lies in the false perception that delegation weakens control or quality. Delegation is not about relinquishing responsibility but about empowering others and creating space for strategic leadership. Without it, growth and efficiency become impossible.

YOUR SOLUTION

1. **Shift Your Mindset:** Recognize that delegation is a tool for growth, not a sign of weakness.
2. **Start Small:** Begin by delegating less critical tasks to build trust in your team.
3. **Set Clear Expectations:** Provide detailed instructions and desired outcomes to ensure alignment.
4. **Empower Your Team:** Give team members the tools, training, and autonomy needed to succeed.
5. **Focus on Leadership:** Use the time saved to focus on strategic decision-making and growth opportunities.

SCRIPTURE REFERENCE

"Two are better than one, because they have a good return for their labor: If either of them falls down, one can help the other up." (Ecclesiastes 4:9-10)
This verse emphasizes the strength and success that come from collaboration and shared effort.

CLOSING THOUGHT

Fearing delegation doesn't protect your business—it limits it. By trusting others and empowering them to contribute, you create opportunities for growth and efficiency. What tasks are you holding onto that someone else could handle? Start small, and watch how delegation strengthens your business and frees you to focus on what matters most.

Problem 12: Believing Your Way Is the Only Way

How rigid thinking stifles innovation and collaboration.

Do you insist that your methods are the only effective way to achieve success? Many people, especially leaders, struggle with a fixed mindset that resists alternative ideas or approaches. This rigidity can stifle creativity, alienate team members, and prevent your business or career from reaching its full potential. The problem isn't your expertise—it's your unwillingness to consider other perspectives.

SUBCONSCIOUS INFLUENCES

Think about Ryan, a manager who micromanages his team because he believes his methods are superior. His *beliefs* that others lack his level of expertise make him reluctant to accept new ideas. Past *memories* of failed group projects create a *bias* against collaboration, while his *fear* of losing control makes him resistant to change.

Ryan's *assumptions* that alternative approaches will lead to inefficiency prevent him from experimenting with new strategies. Motivated by a desire to maintain his reputation for excellence, he *expects* that sticking to what he knows is the safest path forward. These subconscious patterns limit his team's innovation and morale, leaving him stuck in outdated methods.

ROOT CAUSE

The root of this problem lies in overvaluing personal expertise and undervaluing collaboration. Success often requires combining perspectives, adapting to change, and being open to new possibilities. Rigid thinking prevents growth and alienates others who might bring valuable contributions.

27

YOUR SOLUTION

1. **Seek Input:** Regularly ask for feedback and ideas from colleagues, employees, or peers.
2. **Practice Flexibility:** Experiment with different approaches, even if they initially feel uncomfortable.
3. **Value Collaboration:** Recognize the strength in diversity of thought and the innovation it can bring.
4. **Learn From Mistakes:** Accept that trying new methods may include failures that offer valuable lessons.
5. **Empower Others:** Encourage team members to take ownership of tasks and contribute their perspectives.

SCRIPTURE REFERENCE

"Where there is no guidance, a people falls, but in an abundance of counselors there is safety." (Proverbs 11:14) This verse highlights the importance of seeking input and collaboration for success and stability.

CLOSING THOUGHT

Believing your way is the only way limits both your growth and the contributions of those around you. By embracing alternative ideas and collaborating with others, you open the door to innovation, efficiency, and stronger relationships. What perspective or approach have you been resisting, and how can you begin to explore it today? Remember, growth thrives on openness.

Problem 13: Overestimating Immediate Success

How unrealistic expectations prevent long-term growth.

Do you expect immediate results from your efforts, only to feel frustrated when success doesn't come quickly? Many people set unrealistic timelines for their goals, believing that hard work should pay off right away. When results don't align with these expectations, they often give up too soon. The problem isn't your ambition—it's your lack of patience and persistence.

SUBCONSCIOUS INFLUENCES

Consider Jasmine, who started a small business with big dreams but abandoned it within a year because it didn't generate significant profits. Her *beliefs* that success should come quickly were shaped by stories of overnight success in the media. These *memories* reinforced a *bias* toward expecting fast rewards without recognizing the effort and time behind sustained growth.

Jasmine's *fear* of failure leads her to avoid doubling down when results are slow, while her *assumptions* that effort equals immediate success prevent her from focusing on the long term. Motivated by a desire for validation, she *expects* to see instant results as proof of her capabilities. These influences cause her to abandon potentially fruitful opportunities before they have time to mature.

ROOT CAUSE

The root of this problem lies in unrealistic expectations about the timeline for success. Many people fail to recognize that significant achievements are often the result of sustained effort over months or even years. Impatience often leads to abandoning goals that could have yielded great rewards with consistency and time.

YOUR SOLUTION

1. **Set Realistic Goals:** Break your long-term objectives into smaller milestones to track progress over time.
2. **Embrace the Process:** Focus on learning and improving as you work toward success, rather than fixating solely on results.
3. **Develop Patience:** Remind yourself that lasting success often takes longer than expected.
4. **Stay Consistent:** Commit to regular, deliberate actions even when progress feels slow.
5. **Reframe Challenges:** View obstacles as opportunities to grow and refine your approach rather than as reasons to quit.

SCRIPTURE REFERENCE

"Let us not grow weary of doing good, for in due season we will reap, if we do not give up." (Galatians 6:9)
This verse reminds you that persistence and faith are essential to achieving long-term success.

CLOSING THOUGHT

Overestimating immediate success can lead to unnecessary frustration and missed opportunities. By adopting a long-term mindset and embracing the journey, you can build resilience and set yourself up for sustainable growth. What goal have you been tempted to abandon too quickly? Take a step back, adjust your expectations, and recommit to the process today.

Problem 14: Avoiding Feedback From Others

How ignoring constructive input stifles growth and innovation.

Do you resist asking for feedback or dismiss it when it's offered? Many people view constructive criticism as judgment rather than an opportunity for growth. Avoiding feedback may protect your ego, but it limits your ability to learn, improve, and succeed. The problem isn't the feedback—it's your reluctance to embrace it.

SUBCONSCIOUS INFLUENCES

Consider Brian, a business owner who insists on making every decision without consulting his team. His **beliefs** that he knows best prevent him from seeking input. Past **memories** of being harshly criticized create a **bias** against feedback, making him view it as an attack.

Brian's **fear** of appearing weak stops him from asking for advice, while his **assumptions** that others won't understand his vision keep him isolated. Motivated by the desire to maintain control, he **expects** to figure out solutions on his own. These subconscious influences leave him disconnected from valuable insights that could improve his business.

ROOT CAUSE

The root of this problem lies in the inability to separate constructive feedback from personal failure. When feedback is perceived as threatening, it's easy to dismiss it entirely. However, avoiding input from others robs you of perspectives that could illuminate blind spots and lead to better results.

YOUR SOLUTION

1. **Reframe Feedback:** View criticism as an opportunity to grow, not a reflection of your worth.
2. **Ask for Input:** Seek feedback regularly from trusted colleagues, mentors, or clients.
3. **Listen Actively:** Focus on understanding the feedback without immediately reacting defensively.
4. **Evaluate Suggestions:** Identify actionable insights and implement them incrementally.
5. **Express Gratitude:** Thank those who provide feedback, even when it's challenging to hear.

SCRIPTURE REFERENCE

"Plans fail for lack of counsel, but with many advisers they succeed." (Proverbs 15:22)
This verse emphasizes the value of collaboration and seeking wisdom from others to achieve success.

CLOSING THOUGHT

Avoiding feedback limits your ability to grow and adapt. By embracing constructive criticism, you can identify blind spots, refine your strategies, and reach new heights. What feedback have you been avoiding, and how could it help you move forward? Remember, the insights you resist may be the key to your next breakthrough.

Problem 15: Focusing on Competition Instead of Value

How comparing yourself to others holds you back from true success.

Do you spend more time worrying about your competition than focusing on what you offer? Many people fixate on outperforming others, which can lead to a lack of clarity about their own strengths and value. The problem isn't competition—it's letting it overshadow your unique contribution.

SUBCONSCIOUS INFLUENCES

Take Claire, a small business owner who constantly monitors her competitors' every move. Her *beliefs* that success is about "beating the competition" distract her from improving her products. Past *memories* of being compared to others growing up reinforce a *bias* toward measuring her worth through competition.

Claire's *fear* of being left behind keeps her focused on imitation rather than innovation, while her *assumptions* that customers only care about the competition prevent her from building her unique brand. Motivated by a desire to "win," Claire *expects* that mimicking others will lead to success. These subconscious influences keep her trapped in a reactive cycle, rather than allowing her to create genuine value.

ROOT CAUSE

The root of this problem lies in prioritizing competition over authenticity. When you constantly compare yourself to others, you lose sight of what makes you unique. This reactive approach stifles creativity and leads to chasing trends rather than creating meaningful offerings.

YOUR SOLUTION

1. **Focus on Your Strengths:** Identify what sets you apart and double down on your unique value.
2. **Understand Your Audience:** Prioritize what your customers or clients truly need over what others are doing.
3. **Limit Comparisons:** Reduce the time spent analyzing competitors and redirect it toward innovation.
4. **Embrace Collaboration:** Build relationships with others in your field to learn and grow together, rather than competing.
5. **Celebrate Progress:** Measure your success against your own goals, not someone else's milestones.

SCRIPTURE REFERENCE

"Each one should test their own actions. Then they can take pride in themselves alone, without comparing themselves to someone else." (Galatians 6:4)

This verse reminds you to focus on your journey and accomplishments, rather than competing with others.

CLOSING THOUGHT

Focusing on competition instead of value can leave you chasing others' success instead of building your own. By shifting your attention to your strengths and the needs of your audience, you can create lasting impact and fulfillment. What steps can you take today to center your efforts on value rather than comparison? True success comes from authenticity, not rivalry.

RELATIONSHIP PROBLEMS

Problem 16: Fearing Vulnerability Leads to Rejection

How guarding your emotions hinders deep connections.

Do you avoid opening up to others because you fear being judged or rejected? Many people hold back their true feelings and thoughts, assuming vulnerability will make them appear weak. While this may protect you from perceived risks, it also keeps you from building meaningful relationships. The problem isn't vulnerability—it's your fear of it.

SUBCONSCIOUS INFLUENCES

Consider James, who keeps his emotions tightly guarded, even with close friends. His **beliefs** that showing vulnerability is a sign of weakness stem from his upbringing in a family that discouraged emotional expression. Past **memories** of being mocked for sharing his feelings reinforce a **bias** against emotional openness.

James's **fear** of being misunderstood leads him to avoid difficult conversations, while his **assumptions** that others won't accept his true self create emotional walls. Motivated by the desire to appear strong, he **expects** rejection whenever he reveals his feelings. These influences leave him isolated, preventing deeper connections with others.

ROOT CAUSE

The root of this problem lies in equating vulnerability with weakness. True strength comes from authenticity and the courage to share your emotions, even when it feels risky. Avoiding vulnerability keeps you from forming the trust and connection that relationships require.

> **YOUR SOLUTION**
>
> 1. **Challenge Your Beliefs:** Reflect on moments when vulnerability led to understanding or growth.
> 2. **Start Small:** Share your feelings in safe, low-stakes situations to build confidence.
> 3. **Reframe Vulnerability:** View it as a strength that deepens relationships, not a flaw.
> 4. **Practice Active Listening:** Create a space for others to be vulnerable, which often encourages mutual openness.
> 5. **Seek Support:** Surround yourself with people who value authenticity and emotional honesty.

SCRIPTURE REFERENCE

"Carry each other's burdens, and in this way, you will fulfill the law of Christ." (Galatians 6:2)
This verse reminds you that sharing and supporting one another's struggles is a key part of building strong, meaningful connections.

CLOSING THOUGHT

Fearing vulnerability leads to shallow interactions and missed opportunities for trust and intimacy. By embracing emotional openness, you can foster deeper relationships and experience the support and connection you truly need. What feelings or thoughts are you holding back, and how might sharing them strengthen your relationships? True connection starts with courage.

Problem 17: Believing Love Should Be Effortless

How unrealistic expectations can strain relationships.

Do you believe that love should come naturally and require little work? Many people hold onto the idea that true love is effortless, assuming that challenges mean the relationship is flawed. This mindset often leads to disappointment and a lack of investment in nurturing deeper connections. The problem isn't the challenges—it's the belief that love doesn't require effort.

SUBCONSCIOUS INFLUENCES

Take Emma, who struggles in her marriage because she expects her partner to anticipate her needs without communication. Her *beliefs* about love being instinctual come from romanticized portrayals in media. Past *memories* of seeing her parents avoid conflict create a *bias* against addressing issues openly.

Emma's *fear* of seeming demanding keeps her from expressing her needs, while her *assumptions* that love should "just work" prevent her from seeking solutions. Motivated by the desire to maintain harmony, she *expects* that love will thrive on its own, leaving her frustrated when problems arise. These influences cause Emma to overlook the importance of mutual effort and communication.

ROOT CAUSE

The root of this problem lies in the misconception that love is self-sustaining. Relationships require intentional effort, communication, and compromise to grow. Without this investment, even the strongest connections can falter.

1. **Redefine Love:** Understand that love is an ongoing choice, not just a feeling.
2. **Communicate Openly:** Share your needs, concerns, and desires with your partner regularly.
3. **Embrace Conflict:** View disagreements as opportunities to understand and grow closer.
4. **Invest Time and Energy:** Prioritize quality time, shared activities, and acts of care.
5. **Be Patient:** Recognize that building and maintaining love takes consistent effort over time.

SCRIPTURE REFERENCE

"Above all, love each other deeply, because love covers over a multitude of sins." (1 Peter 4:8)
This verse highlights the depth of love and the intentional effort required to sustain it.

CLOSING THOUGHT

Believing that love should be effortless can lead to frustration and disconnection. By embracing the idea that love requires effort and commitment, you can build stronger, more fulfilling relationships. What step can you take today to invest in your connection with someone you care about? Remember, love grows through intentional care.

Problem 18: Allowing Past Hurts to Define Current Trust

How unresolved pain sabotages your relationships.

Do you struggle to fully trust others because of past experiences where you were hurt or betrayed? Many people carry emotional scars into new relationships, letting old wounds influence how they connect with others. While this can feel protective, it often prevents genuine intimacy. The problem isn't trust itself—it's allowing past pain to dictate your present relationships.

SUBCONSCIOUS INFLUENCES

Consider Sarah, who keeps her friends and partner at arm's length because of a previous betrayal by a close friend. Her *beliefs* that trusting others leads to hurt keep her guarded. Past *memories* of being let down reinforce a *bias* that people are inherently untrustworthy.

Sarah's *fear* of being vulnerable again stops her from building deeper connections, while her *assumptions* that others will repeat past behaviors prevent her from giving new people a chance. Motivated by self-protection, she *expects* that trust will inevitably lead to disappointment. These influences create a cycle where Sarah isolates herself, unable to heal and move forward.

ROOT CAUSE

The root of this problem lies in unhealed emotional wounds. When you let past experiences shape your perspective on all future relationships, you limit your ability to trust and connect. Healing requires confronting and processing old pain, not projecting it onto new situations.

YOUR SOLUTION

1. **Acknowledge the Pain:** Reflect on the specific incidents that caused you to lose trust.
2. **Separate the Past From the Present:** Recognize that new relationships are not defined by old ones.
3. **Communicate Openly:** Share your concerns with trusted people who can support your healing.
4. **Take Small Steps:** Gradually rebuild trust by allowing yourself to be vulnerable in safe situations.
5. **Seek Professional Help:** Work with a counselor or therapist to address deeper wounds.

SCRIPTURE REFERENCE

"Be kind and compassionate to one another, forgiving each other, just as in Christ God forgave you." (Ephesians 4:32)
This verse emphasizes the importance of forgiveness and compassion in overcoming past hurts.

CLOSING THOUGHT

Allowing past hurts to define your current trust creates barriers to the meaningful connections you deserve. By acknowledging your pain and taking steps toward healing, you can rebuild trust and open yourself to deeper relationships. What past hurt is holding you back, and how can you begin to release its grip on your life? Remember, healing starts with forgiveness and courage.

Problem 19: Assuming Communication Happens Naturally

How neglecting intentional dialogue weakens relationships.

Do you believe that good communication will happen on its own without effort? Many people assume that strong relationships don't require deliberate conversations, expecting others to intuitively understand their thoughts and feelings. This mindset often leads to misunderstandings, frustration, and disconnection. The problem isn't the lack of communication—it's assuming it doesn't need to be cultivated.

SUBCONSCIOUS INFLUENCES

Think about Jason, who feels distant from his partner because they no longer talk like they used to. His *beliefs* that love alone should ensure communication keep him from making intentional efforts to connect. Past *memories* of effortless conversations early in the relationship reinforce a *bias* that communication doesn't require work.

Jason's *fear* of being misunderstood stops him from expressing deeper emotions, while his *assumptions* that his partner should "just know" what he's thinking lead to resentment. Motivated by a desire to avoid conflict, he *expects* communication to happen without effort, leaving both parties feeling unheard. These subconscious patterns create a cycle of distance and dissatisfaction.

ROOT CAUSE

The root of this problem lies in misunderstanding the role of intentionality in communication. Strong relationships require consistent effort to create meaningful dialogue, foster understanding, and resolve conflicts. Assuming communication will happen naturally often leads to emotional disconnects.

YOUR SOLUTION

1. **Prioritize Conversations:** Set aside time for meaningful dialogue with loved ones.
2. **Express Your Needs Clearly:** Communicate your thoughts and feelings without expecting others to guess.
3. **Practice Active Listening:** Focus on understanding the other person's perspective without interrupting or judging.
4. **Ask Questions:** Show genuine curiosity about the other person's experiences, thoughts, and feelings.
5. **Address Issues Early:** Don't wait for misunderstandings to escalate before discussing them openly.

SCRIPTURE REFERENCE

"My dear brothers and sisters, take note of this: Everyone should be quick to listen, slow to speak, and slow to become angry." (James 1:19)
This verse highlights the importance of listening and thoughtful communication in building strong relationships.

CLOSING THOUGHT

Assuming communication happens naturally can lead to unnecessary conflict and emotional distance. By prioritizing intentional conversations and practicing active listening, you can create deeper connections and understanding. What relationship in your life could benefit from more intentional communication? Start today by opening the door to meaningful dialogue.

Problem 20: Motivating Actions Through Control, Not Understanding

How forcing outcomes damages relationships and trust.

Do you try to control others' actions to get the results you want? Many people believe that exerting control is the best way to achieve harmony, but this often leads to resistance, resentment, and broken trust. The problem isn't wanting cooperation—it's using control instead of understanding to achieve it.

SUBCONSCIOUS INFLUENCES

Consider Lisa, a mother who tightly manages every aspect of her teenage daughter's life. Her *beliefs* that control equals care come from her childhood, where structure was heavily enforced. Past *memories* of her own mistakes as a teen create a *bias* toward micromanaging to prevent similar outcomes.

Lisa's *fear* of things going wrong leads her to enforce strict rules without discussion, while her *assumptions* that she knows best alienate her daughter. Motivated by the desire to protect, Lisa *expects* compliance without considering her daughter's feelings or perspective. These subconscious influences create tension and erode the trust between them.

ROOT CAUSE

The root of this problem lies in equating control with care. Genuine connection requires understanding others' perspectives, not dictating their actions. When control replaces communication, it undermines trust and mutual respect, leading to conflict and distance.

Your Solution

1. **Shift From Control to Understanding:** Focus on listening and learning about the other person's needs and feelings.
2. **Communicate Openly:** Explain your concerns and goals, and invite input to create mutual solutions.
3. **Respect Autonomy:** Allow others to make their own choices, even if they differ from your preferences.
4. **Focus on Collaboration:** Work together to achieve outcomes that benefit everyone involved.
5. **Reflect on Your Motivations:** Examine whether your actions stem from fear or a genuine desire to help.

SCRIPTURE REFERENCE

"Do to others as you would have them do to you." (Luke 6:31)

This verse emphasizes the importance of treating others with respect and empathy, fostering mutual understanding.

CLOSING THOUGHT

Motivating actions through control may bring short-term compliance but often damages trust and long-term relationships. By focusing on understanding and collaboration, you can foster deeper connections and achieve lasting harmony. Who in your life could benefit from more understanding and less control? Start today by opening the door to meaningful dialogue.

PERSONAL GROWTH PROBLEMS

Problem 21: Fearing Change Will Make You Lose Yourself

How resisting transformation hinders your personal growth.

Do you avoid change because you're afraid it will alter who you are? Many people cling to their current identity, fearing that growth or transformation might distance them from their values, relationships, or sense of self. The problem isn't change itself—it's the fear of what it might take away.

SUBCONSCIOUS INFLUENCES

Take Rachel, who dreams of switching careers but stays in her current role because of the uncertainty that comes with change. Her **beliefs** that stability equals safety hold her back from taking risks. Past **memories** of failed attempts at personal improvement create a **bias** against trying again.

Rachel's **fear** of losing her identity as someone dependable keeps her from pursuing her dreams. Her **assumptions** that change requires abandoning what she values most prevent her from moving forward, while her **expectations** that growth will disrupt her life reinforce her resistance. These subconscious influences keep Rachel stuck, even as she feels unfulfilled.

ROOT CAUSE

The root of this problem lies in the misconception that growth means losing your core self. Change, when approached with intention, enhances who you are rather than erasing it. Resisting transformation often results in stagnation and missed opportunities for self-discovery.

> **YOUR SOLUTION**
>
> 1. **Reframe Change:** View change as a way to expand and refine your identity, not replace it.
> 2. **Clarify Your Values:** Identify what matters most to you and use it as a guide during transitions.
> 3. **Start Small:** Embrace manageable changes to build confidence in your ability to adapt.
> 4. **Seek Support:** Surround yourself with people who encourage and guide you through growth.
> 5. **Reflect on Your Journey:** Regularly assess how change has positively impacted your life to build trust in the process.

SCRIPTURE REFERENCE

"Therefore, if anyone is in Christ, the new creation has come: The old has gone, the new is here!" (2 Corinthians 5:17) This verse reminds you that transformation brings renewal and growth, not loss.

CLOSING THOUGHT

Fearing that change will make you lose yourself keeps you from discovering your full potential. By embracing transformation as a tool for growth, you can align your actions with your values and find greater fulfillment. What change have you been avoiding, and how could it enhance who you are? Remember, growth strengthens your identity—it doesn't erase it.

Problem 22: Associating Failure With Personal Deficiency

How internalizing mistakes keeps you from growing.

Do you view failure as a reflection of your worth? Many people believe that failing at something means they are inherently flawed, which can lead to self-doubt and hesitation to try again. This mindset doesn't just hold you back—it keeps you stuck in a cycle of fear and avoidance. The problem isn't failure—it's how you interpret it.

SUBCONSCIOUS INFLUENCES

Consider Michael, who avoids starting a side business after his first venture didn't succeed. His *beliefs* that failure defines his ability were shaped by past experiences of being criticized for mistakes. These *memories* created a *bias* toward equating setbacks with personal inadequacy.

Michael's *fear* of reliving the pain of failure stops him from taking new risks. His *assumptions* that success must be immediate discourage perseverance, and his *expectations* of being judged further reinforce his reluctance to try again. These subconscious influences keep Michael trapped in self-doubt, preventing him from learning and growing.

ROOT CAUSE

The root of this problem lies in internalizing failure rather than viewing it as a learning opportunity. When you tie your worth to your outcomes, you limit your capacity to grow and adapt. Failure isn't an end—it's a stepping stone to success when approached with the right mindset.

YOUR SOLUTION

1. **Reframe Failure:** See mistakes as feedback and a natural part of growth, not as a reflection of your value.
2. **Separate Identity From Outcomes:** Recognize that your worth isn't defined by your achievements or setbacks.
3. **Learn From Mistakes:** Reflect on what went wrong and identify actionable lessons for future attempts.
4. **Celebrate Resilience:** Acknowledge your courage to try, even if the results weren't what you hoped for.
5. **Keep Moving Forward:** Use failure as motivation to refine your approach and keep striving for success.

SCRIPTURE REFERENCE

"For though the righteous fall seven times, they rise again, but the wicked stumble when calamity strikes." (Proverbs 24:16)

This verse highlights the resilience that comes from getting back up after failure, emphasizing perseverance over perfection.

CLOSING THOUGHT

Associating failure with personal deficiency keeps you stuck in fear and self-doubt. By separating your worth from your outcomes and viewing failure as a tool for growth, you can build resilience and achieve greater success. What failure has been holding you back, and how can you turn it into an opportunity to grow? Remember, failure isn't final—it's part of the journey.

Problem 23: Assuming Success Happens Without Struggle

How unrealistic expectations hinder your progress.

Do you believe that success should come easily if you're on the right path? Many people assume that struggle or setbacks mean they're failing, leading to frustration and a lack of perseverance. This mindset keeps you from embracing the challenges necessary for growth and achievement. The problem isn't the struggle—it's the belief that success shouldn't involve it.

SUBCONSCIOUS INFLUENCES

Take Lisa, who abandoned her dream of becoming an artist after her first gallery rejection. Her *beliefs* that talent alone should ensure success lead her to avoid trying again. Past *memories* of being praised for effortless achievements reinforce a *bias* against pursuing goals that require sustained effort.

Lisa's *fear* of failure prevents her from embracing the hard work needed to improve, while her *assumptions* that successful people don't struggle create unrealistic standards. Motivated by a desire for instant validation, she *expects* success to come easily or not at all. These subconscious influences stop Lisa from persevering through the challenges that lead to mastery and fulfillment.

ROOT CAUSE

The root of this problem lies in conflating struggle with failure. Success is rarely linear, and growth often requires persistence through difficulties. Viewing challenges as evidence of being on the wrong path limits your resilience and ability to adapt.

> **YOUR SOLUTION**
>
> 1. **Embrace the Process:** Recognize that struggle is a natural part of growth and success.
> 2. **Redefine Struggle:** View challenges as opportunities to learn and improve, not as roadblocks.
> 3. **Set Realistic Expectations:** Understand that progress often involves setbacks and requires time.
> 4. **Celebrate Effort:** Focus on the work you put in, not just the results, to build confidence.
> 5. **Seek Support:** Surround yourself with people who encourage you to persevere through challenges.

SCRIPTURE REFERENCE

"Not only so, but we also glory in our sufferings, because we know that suffering produces perseverance; perseverance, character; and character, hope." (Romans 5:3-4)
This verse reminds you that struggles lead to growth, resilience, and ultimately success.

CLOSING THOUGHT

Assuming success happens without struggle sets you up for disappointment and limits your potential. By embracing challenges as part of the journey, you can develop the resilience needed to achieve your goals. What struggle are you facing right now, and how can you use it to grow? Remember, success is built through perseverance, not perfection.

Problem 24: Clinging to Comfort Zones

How avoiding discomfort limits your personal growth.

Do you stay in your comfort zone, avoiding challenges that push you to grow? Many people believe that stability and predictability are the keys to happiness, but this mindset often leads to stagnation and missed opportunities. The problem isn't the comfort itself—it's refusing to step beyond it.

SUBCONSCIOUS INFLUENCES

Consider Mark, a talented writer who avoids submitting his work for publication out of fear of rejection. His **beliefs** that staying safe is better than risking failure keep him from pursuing opportunities. Past **memories** of being criticized for his work create a **bias** against stepping into the unknown.

Mark's **fear** of failure prevents him from taking risks, while his **assumptions** that success comes only with certainty keep him stuck. Motivated by the desire to avoid discomfort, he **expects** that staying in his current routine will lead to eventual growth, even though it hasn't. These subconscious patterns hold him back from exploring his full potential.

ROOT CAUSE

The root of this problem lies in equating comfort with safety and growth with risk. Growth requires stepping into new and unfamiliar experiences, which can feel unsettling but ultimately lead to greater opportunities and fulfillment.

YOUR SOLUTION

1. **Challenge Comfort:** Identify areas where staying comfortable is limiting your progress.
2. **Take Small Risks:** Start with manageable challenges to build confidence in facing discomfort.
3. **Focus on Growth:** Remind yourself that discomfort is a sign of progress, not failure.
4. **Learn From Setbacks:** View failures as lessons that bring you closer to your goals.
5. **Seek Encouragement:** Surround yourself with people who inspire you to stretch beyond your limits.

SCRIPTURE REFERENCE

"Enlarge the place of your tent, stretch your tent curtains wide, do not hold back; lengthen your cords, strengthen your stakes." (Isaiah 54:2)

This verse encourages you to expand your boundaries and embrace new opportunities.

CLOSING THOUGHT

Clinging to your comfort zone may feel safe, but it often keeps you from achieving your greatest potential. By embracing discomfort and stepping into new challenges, you can unlock personal growth and fulfillment. What step can you take today to move beyond your comfort zone? Remember, growth begins where comfort ends.

Problem 25: Believing Growth Has an Expiration Date

How limiting beliefs about age or timing hold you back.

Do you think it's too late to pursue your goals or grow in new ways? Many people believe that personal growth and success are only achievable within a specific timeframe, and if they've missed that window, there's no point in trying. This mindset doesn't just limit your opportunities—it prevents you from exploring your full potential. The problem isn't your age—it's the belief that growth has a deadline.

SUBCONSCIOUS INFLUENCES

Think of Laura, who always wanted to go back to school but feels she's "too old" to start over. Her *beliefs* that certain milestones must happen by a specific age were shaped by societal expectations. Past *memories* of being compared to others who achieved success earlier create a *bias* that it's now "too late" for her.

Laura's *fear* of being judged for starting something new keeps her from taking action, while her *assumptions* that younger people are more capable discourage her efforts. Motivated by a desire to avoid failure or embarrassment, she *expects* that growth is no longer possible for her. These subconscious influences keep her stuck in a cycle of regret and inaction.

ROOT CAUSE

The root of this problem lies in societal and personal narratives that equate growth and success with youth or timing. True growth can happen at any stage of life, as long as you're willing to pursue it. Limiting yourself to a perceived "deadline" closes doors that could lead to meaningful accomplishments.

YOUR SOLUTION

1. **Redefine Success:** Understand that growth is a lifelong process, not confined to a specific timeframe.
2. **Focus on the Present:** Shift your attention from what you haven't done to what you can do now.
3. **Learn From Others:** Seek out stories of people who achieved success or started new ventures later in life.
4. **Take Small Steps:** Begin with manageable actions to build momentum and confidence.
5. **Challenge Negative Narratives:** Replace thoughts of "too late" with "just in time" and embrace new opportunities.

SCRIPTURE REFERENCE

"They will still bear fruit in old age, they will stay fresh and green." (Psalm 92:14)

This verse reminds you that growth and purpose can flourish at any stage of life.

CLOSING THOUGHT

Believing that growth has an expiration date limits your ability to embrace new opportunities and redefine your potential. By shifting your mindset and taking small, consistent steps, you can achieve meaningful progress no matter where you are in life. What goal have you put off because you think it's too late? Start today—it's never too late to grow.

PARENTING PROBLEMS

Problem 26: Assuming Control Equals Good Parenting

How over-managing your child's life stifles their growth.

Do you believe that being a good parent means controlling every aspect of your child's life? Many parents think that micromanaging their children's decisions ensures success and protection. However, this approach can undermine a child's independence, decision-making skills, and confidence. The problem isn't your care—it's how control replaces guidance.

SUBCONSCIOUS INFLUENCES

Consider Jenna, a mother who closely monitors her son's every move, from his homework to his social life. Her *beliefs* that a parent's role is to prevent mistakes stem from her upbringing, where strict control was the norm. Past *memories* of her own failures create a *bias* that mistakes should be avoided at all costs.

Jenna's *fear* of her child experiencing pain or failure drives her need for control, while her *assumptions* that her child isn't ready to make decisions discourage autonomy. Motivated by love and protection, she *expects* compliance rather than collaboration, creating tension and dependency. These subconscious influences hinder her child's ability to learn and grow.

ROOT CAUSE

The root of this problem lies in equating control with care. While parents want the best for their children, over-managing prevents them from developing the skills and resilience needed to

55

navigate life's challenges. True guidance involves trust, support, and allowing children to grow through experience.

YOUR SOLUTION

1. **Shift From Control to Guidance:** Focus on teaching and supporting rather than directing every decision.
2. **Encourage Autonomy:** Allow your child to make age-appropriate decisions, even if it means learning from mistakes.
3. **Communicate Openly:** Discuss expectations and consequences collaboratively to build mutual understanding.
4. **Celebrate Effort Over Perfection:** Focus on growth and learning rather than outcomes.
5. **Trust Their Growth:** Recognize that challenges help your child develop resilience and confidence.

SCRIPTURE REFERENCE

"Start children off on the way they should go, and even when they are old they will not turn from it." (Proverbs 22:6) This verse highlights the importance of laying a strong foundation while allowing children to grow independently.

CLOSING THOUGHT

Assuming control equals good parenting may feel protective, but it can limit your child's ability to grow and thrive. By shifting your focus to guidance and trust, you can empower your child to become confident and capable. What areas of your child's life can you release control over to encourage their growth? Remember, parenting is about preparing your child for independence, not perfection.

Problem 27: Projecting Your Own Fears Onto Your Children

How your insecurities can limit their potential.

Do you find yourself discouraging your child from pursuing certain goals or interests because of your own fears or past experiences? Many parents unknowingly project their insecurities onto their children, believing they're protecting them from harm. The problem isn't your care—it's how your fears influence their choices.

SUBCONSCIOUS INFLUENCES

Consider Mark, a father who discourages his daughter from studying art because he struggled financially as an artist. His *beliefs* that financial stability is the ultimate measure of success drive his advice. Past *memories* of his own career failures create a *bias* that certain paths will inevitably lead to hardship.

Mark's *fear* of his daughter experiencing the same struggles leads him to push her toward a safer career, while his *assumptions* that she won't succeed in the arts limit her potential. Motivated by love and a desire to protect her, he *expects* her to follow his advice, even if it conflicts with her passions. These subconscious patterns unintentionally stifle her growth and creativity.

ROOT CAUSE

The root of this problem lies in projecting unresolved fears onto your child's future. While it's natural to want the best for them, their path is not yours. Focusing on your insecurities rather than their potential can prevent them from exploring their unique talents and opportunities.

1. **Recognize Your Fears:** Reflect on whether your concerns stem from their reality or your past experiences.
2. **Focus on Their Strengths:** Encourage your child to pursue their interests and talents, even if they differ from your expectations.
3. **Communicate Openly:** Share your concerns without discouraging their dreams, and invite them to express their goals.
4. **Encourage Resilience:** Teach them how to navigate challenges rather than avoiding them entirely.
5. **Support Their Growth:** Trust their ability to learn, adapt, and succeed in their own way.

SCRIPTURE REFERENCE

"For God gave us a spirit not of fear but of power and love and self-control." (2 Timothy 1:7)
This verse reminds you to approach parenting with faith and courage, not fear.

CLOSING THOUGHT

Projecting your fears onto your children limits their ability to explore, grow, and fulfill their potential. By focusing on their strengths and dreams instead of your insecurities, you can support them in becoming their best selves. What fears are you projecting onto your child, and how can you release them today? Remember, your role is to guide, not define, their journey.

Problem 28: Allowing Biases to Shape Discipline Methods

How unexamined beliefs affect how you guide your children.

Do you ever react to your child's behavior based on assumptions rather than understanding their unique needs? Many parents unintentionally allow biases from their upbringing or cultural norms to influence how they discipline their children. While these methods may feel familiar or justified, they often fail to address the root causes of behavior. The problem isn't discipline—it's relying on unexamined biases to guide it.

SUBCONSCIOUS INFLUENCES

Think of Sarah, who often raises her voice at her son because that's how her parents handled misbehavior. Her **beliefs** that strict discipline equals good parenting stem from her upbringing. Past **memories** of being punished harshly create a **bias** that fear is necessary for obedience.

Sarah's **assumptions** that her child understands her expectations, even when she hasn't clearly communicated them, lead to frustration. Motivated by a desire to maintain control, she **expects** immediate compliance without considering her child's perspective. These subconscious influences result in ineffective discipline methods that strain their relationship.

ROOT CAUSE

The root of this problem lies in using inherited or unexamined approaches to discipline rather than adapting methods to your child's needs. Effective discipline requires empathy, clear communication, and a willingness to question your own assumptions about what works.

YOUR SOLUTION

1. **Reflect on Your Approach:** Identify how your discipline methods were shaped by your upbringing and whether they align with your values.
2. **Understand Your Child:** Consider their unique personality, age, and needs when addressing behavior.
3. **Communicate Expectations:** Clearly explain rules and consequences to avoid misunderstandings.
4. **Practice Empathy:** Respond to misbehavior with understanding rather than anger or frustration.
5. **Adapt and Learn:** Be open to adjusting your methods as you learn what works best for your child.

SCRIPTURE REFERENCE

"Fathers, do not exasperate your children; instead, bring them up in the training and instruction of the Lord."
(Ephesians 6:4)
This verse encourages parents to discipline with care and guidance rather than frustration or harshness.

CLOSING THOUGHT

Allowing biases to shape discipline methods can create unnecessary tension and prevent meaningful growth for both you and your child. By examining your approach and tailoring it to your child's needs, you can foster trust, understanding, and effective guidance. What assumptions are driving your discipline methods, and how can you replace them with empathy and intentionality? Remember, discipline is most effective when it's rooted in love and understanding.

Problem 29: Failing to Adapt to Your Child's Growth

How sticking to outdated parenting methods stifles your child's development.

Do you find yourself using the same parenting strategies as your child grows, even when they no longer seem effective? Many parents struggle to adjust their approach as their children mature, holding onto methods that worked in the past. While consistency is important, failure to adapt can hinder your child's independence and confidence. The problem isn't your guidance—it's your resistance to change.

SUBCONSCIOUS INFLUENCES

Take James, a father who continues to use strict rules for his teenage son, the same rules he used when his son was in elementary school. His *beliefs* that structure is always necessary prevent him from loosening his approach. Past *memories* of rebellion during his own teenage years create a *bias* toward overprotectiveness.

James's *fear* of losing authority keeps him from giving his son more autonomy, while his *assumptions* that his son still needs constant supervision limit opportunities for growth. Motivated by love and concern, he *expects* that maintaining the same level of control will ensure his son's success. These subconscious patterns create tension and discourage open communication.

ROOT CAUSE

The root of this problem lies in treating children as static rather than dynamic individuals. As children grow, their needs, understanding, and abilities evolve. Parenting that doesn't adjust to these changes can stifle their development and strain the parent-child relationship.

SCRIPTURE REFERENCE

"When I was a child, I talked like a child, I thought like a child, I reasoned like a child. When I became a man, I put the ways of childhood behind me." (1 Corinthians 13:11)
This verse reminds you that growth is natural and requires changes in behavior and expectations.

CLOSING THOUGHT

Failing to adapt to your child's growth can lead to frustration and missed opportunities for connection. By evolving your parenting approach, you can empower your child to thrive while maintaining a strong relationship. How can you adjust your guidance to better support your child's current stage of life? Remember, growth requires flexibility—from both you and your child.

Problem 30: Believing Parental Love Is Always Enough

How ignoring practical needs can hinder your child's development.

Do you believe that loving your child unconditionally is all it takes to ensure their success and happiness? While love is essential, it's not a substitute for providing guidance, structure, and resources. The problem isn't your love—it's assuming it's the only thing your child needs to thrive.

SUBCONSCIOUS INFLUENCES

Consider Karen, a single mother who struggles to enforce rules with her teenage daughter because she doesn't want to seem harsh. Her *beliefs* that love alone will keep her daughter on the right path lead her to avoid addressing difficult behaviors. Past *memories* of feeling unloved as a child create a *bias* toward showing affection instead of setting boundaries.

Karen's *fear* of damaging their relationship keeps her from implementing discipline, while her *assumptions* that her daughter will figure things out on her own prevent her from stepping in when needed. Motivated by a desire to be a supportive parent, she *expects* that her love will compensate for the lack of structure. These subconscious influences leave Karen's daughter unprepared for challenges and responsibilities.

ROOT CAUSE

The root of this problem lies in equating love with passivity. While love provides emotional security, children also need discipline, accountability, and practical tools to navigate life. Failing to balance love with structure can hinder their growth and independence.

SCRIPTURE REFERENCE

"Discipline your children, and they will give you peace; they will bring you the delights you desire." (Proverbs 29:17) This verse emphasizes the importance of combining love with guidance and discipline to create a harmonious relationship.

CLOSING THOUGHT

Believing parental love is always enough can leave your child unprepared for life's challenges. By pairing your love with structure, support, and accountability, you can help them develop the skills they need to succeed. What practical needs can you address today to balance love with preparation? Remember, true love empowers growth.

FRIENDSHIP PROBLEMS

Problem 31: Fearing Rejection Prevents True Connection

How avoiding vulnerability keeps friendships shallow.

Do you hold back from being your true self in friendships because you fear rejection? Many people struggle to build meaningful connections, afraid that revealing their flaws or emotions will push others away. The problem isn't your fear—it's allowing it to prevent authentic relationships.

SUBCONSCIOUS INFLUENCES

Consider Josh, who avoids sharing personal struggles with his friends. His *beliefs* that vulnerability equals weakness stem from childhood experiences of being teased for expressing emotions. Past *memories* of being rejected by peers create a *bias* that others will always judge him.

Josh's *fear* of being misunderstood stops him from opening up, while his *assumptions* that his friends wouldn't accept his flaws keep him distant. Motivated by a desire to maintain surface-level harmony, he *expects* rejection if he lets his guard down. These subconscious influences prevent Josh from forming deep, meaningful friendships.

ROOT CAUSE

The root of this problem lies in conflating vulnerability with risk rather than connection. True friendship thrives on honesty and mutual understanding, which can only be achieved by embracing authenticity. Fear of rejection often creates the very isolation you're trying to avoid.

SCRIPTURE REFERENCE

"A friend loves at all times, and a brother is born for a time of adversity." (Proverbs 17:17)
This verse highlights the enduring and supportive nature of true friendships, which thrive on authenticity and trust.

CLOSING THOUGHT

Fearing rejection prevents you from experiencing the depth and support of genuine friendships. By embracing vulnerability and authenticity, you can create stronger, more fulfilling connections. What fear is holding you back from being your true self with a friend? Take a step toward openness today—true connection begins with courage.

Problem 32: Assuming Real Friends Require No Effort

How neglecting your friendships leads to disconnection.

Do you believe that true friends will always understand your absence, no matter how little effort you make to maintain the relationship? Many people assume that genuine friendships are self-sustaining and don't need regular attention. While strong bonds can endure challenges, neglecting them over time often leads to distance and misunderstanding. The problem isn't your friendships—it's the lack of effort you invest in them.

SUBCONSCIOUS INFLUENCES

Think of Carla, who hasn't reached out to her childhood best friend in years but assumes their bond remains unchanged. Her **beliefs** that real friends don't need constant communication come from a culture that values independence over connection. Past **memories** of friendships that seemed effortless create a **bias** that relationships require no work.

Carla's **assumptions** that her friend understands her busy life prevent her from making time to connect, while her **expectations** that the friendship will pick up where it left off lead to disappointment when it doesn't. Motivated by convenience, Carla avoids the intentional effort needed to nurture the bond. These subconscious influences create unintentional distance between her and her friend.

ROOT CAUSE

The root of this problem lies in undervaluing the importance of consistent care in maintaining relationships. Friendships, like any meaningful connection, require effort, communication, and time to thrive. Neglect often leads to unspoken hurt and eventual disconnection.

SCRIPTURE REFERENCE

"Two are better than one, because they have a good return for their labor: If either of them falls down, one can help the other up." (Ecclesiastes 4:9-10)

This verse emphasizes the mutual effort and support required to build and sustain meaningful relationships.

CLOSING THOUGHT

Assuming real friends require no effort can weaken the very bonds you cherish most. By being intentional and consistent in your care, you can nurture deeper and more lasting connections. What friendship have you been neglecting, and how can you show effort today? Remember, strong relationships are built, not assumed.

Problem 33: Believing Past Betrayals Predict Future Bonds

How holding onto distrust prevents you from forming meaningful friendships.

Do you find yourself hesitant to trust new friends because of betrayals in the past? Many people allow the pain of broken friendships to shape their expectations of all future connections. While this can feel like self-protection, it often prevents you from forming meaningful relationships. The problem isn't the betrayal—it's carrying it forward into new bonds.

SUBCONSCIOUS INFLUENCES

Take Lisa, who keeps her friendships superficial after being betrayed by a close friend in college. Her **beliefs** that most people are untrustworthy keep her from opening up. Past **memories** of feeling hurt and vulnerable reinforce a **bias** against trusting others deeply.

Lisa's **fear** of experiencing the same pain stops her from forming new connections, while her **assumptions** that people will always disappoint her lead to emotional walls. Motivated by a desire to avoid risk, she **expects** every new friendship to end in betrayal. These subconscious patterns isolate her, leaving her lonely and disconnected.

ROOT CAUSE

The root of this problem lies in allowing past experiences to dictate your approach to new relationships. While betrayal is painful, projecting it onto future connections robs you of the chance to experience trust, support, and joy in friendships. Healing requires letting go of old wounds and embracing new possibilities.

YOUR SOLUTION

1. **Acknowledge the Hurt:** Reflect on past betrayals and how they've shaped your mindset about trust.
2. **Separate the Past From the Present:** Recognize that new friends are not responsible for past betrayals.
3. **Start Small:** Build trust incrementally by sharing little by little in new relationships.
4. **Forgive and Release:** Let go of resentment toward those who hurt you, freeing yourself from their influence.
5. **Seek Positive Examples:** Surround yourself with people who consistently demonstrate loyalty and care.

SCRIPTURE REFERENCE

"Above all, love each other deeply, because love covers over a multitude of sins." (1 Peter 4:8)
This verse reminds you of the power of love and forgiveness in building and restoring relationships.

CLOSING THOUGHT

Believing past betrayals predict future bonds keeps you trapped in distrust and loneliness. By releasing old wounds and approaching new friendships with openness, you can experience the joy of meaningful connections. What past betrayal are you holding onto, and how can you begin to let it go today? Remember, trust starts with a choice to move forward.

Problem 34: Allowing Jealousy to Poison Relationships

How comparison damages trust and connection with friends.

Do you find yourself feeling envious when a friend achieves something you haven't? Many people struggle with jealousy in friendships, which can create tension, resentment, and even sabotage the relationship. The problem isn't your friend's success—it's your reaction to it.

SUBCONSCIOUS INFLUENCES

Think about Mia, who starts avoiding her best friend after she gets a promotion. Mia's **beliefs** that someone else's gain diminishes her worth lead to feelings of inadequacy. Past **memories** of being overlooked for opportunities reinforce a **bias** that life is a competition.

Mia's **fear** that her friend's success will highlight her own shortcomings drives her to withdraw. Her **assumptions** that their friendship can't survive this imbalance keep her from celebrating her friend's achievements. Motivated by insecurity, Mia **expects** to lose the relationship, which creates unnecessary distance. These subconscious patterns undermine the friendship and harm Mia's self-esteem.

ROOT CAUSE

The root of this problem lies in seeing relationships through the lens of competition rather than connection. Jealousy stems from insecurity and a scarcity mindset, which prevent you from valuing your unique journey. True friendships thrive on support and mutual celebration, not comparison.

YOUR SOLUTION

1. **Acknowledge Your Feelings:** Recognize jealousy when it arises and reflect on its source.
2. **Celebrate Their Success:** Shift your focus from envy to pride in your friend's accomplishments.
3. **Focus on Your Path:** Remind yourself that your journey is unique and not diminished by others' achievements.
4. **Communicate Openly:** Share your feelings with trusted friends to foster understanding and strengthen the bond.
5. **Practice Gratitude:** Regularly reflect on your own successes and blessings to combat a scarcity mindset.

SCRIPTURE REFERENCE

"Rejoice with those who rejoice; mourn with those who mourn." (Romans 12:15)
This verse encourages empathy and shared joy as essential elements of strong relationships.

CLOSING THOUGHT

Allowing jealousy to poison your relationships creates unnecessary distance and pain. By focusing on your own path and celebrating your friends' successes, you can build deeper, more supportive connections. What step can you take today to turn envy into encouragement? Remember, true friendships are built on mutual joy, not competition.

Problem 35: Expecting Others to Always Meet Your Needs

How unrealistic expectations strain friendships.

Do you rely on your friends to meet all your emotional, social, or practical needs? Many people unconsciously place too much responsibility on their friends, expecting them to always be available or to perfectly fulfill their desires. When these expectations go unmet, frustration and disappointment often follow. The problem isn't your friends—it's your unrealistic reliance on them.

SUBCONSCIOUS INFLUENCES

Take Emma, who becomes upset when her best friend doesn't respond to her texts immediately. Her *beliefs* that true friendship means constant availability lead to frustration. Past *memories* of being let down by others create a *bias* toward expecting perfection from her current friendships.

Emma's *fear* of feeling unsupported makes her overly dependent, while her *assumptions* that her friends should always prioritize her needs lead to tension. Motivated by a desire for reassurance, she *expects* her friends to consistently meet her emotional demands. These subconscious patterns strain her relationships and prevent her from seeking balance.

ROOT CAUSE

The root of this problem lies in placing unrealistic expectations on friendships. While friends can provide support and connection, no one person can meet all your needs. Healthy relationships thrive on mutual respect and boundaries, not dependency.

YOUR SOLUTION

1. **Recognize Your Patterns:** Reflect on whether you're placing too much emotional or practical responsibility on your friends.
2. **Diversify Your Support System:** Seek fulfillment through a variety of relationships, interests, and personal growth.
3. **Communicate Clearly:** Share your needs without expecting your friends to intuitively know or always meet them.
4. **Respect Boundaries:** Allow your friends space to prioritize their own needs and responsibilities.
5. **Foster Mutuality:** Focus on giving as much as you receive in the relationship.

SCRIPTURE REFERENCE

"Do to others as you would have them do to you." (Luke 6:31)

This verse emphasizes the importance of treating others with the same consideration and respect your desire.

CLOSING THOUGHT

Expecting others to always meet your needs places undue pressure on friendships, leading to disappointment and tension. By diversifying your sources of support and respecting boundaries, you can foster healthier, more balanced relationships. What expectations are you placing on your friends, and how can you adjust them today? Remember, friendships flourish with mutual respect and understanding.

HEALTH AND WELLNESS PROBLEMS

Problem 36: Believing Fitness Is Only Physical

How ignoring mental and emotional wellness limits your overall health.

Do you think being fit is just about how you look or how much you exercise? Many people focus exclusively on physical fitness, neglecting the mental and emotional aspects of well-being. This narrow perspective can lead to burnout, dissatisfaction, and imbalanced health. The problem isn't your desire for fitness—it's the way you define it.

SUBCONSCIOUS INFLUENCES

Consider Daniel, who spends hours in the gym each week but struggles with stress and anxiety. His *belief* that physical fitness is the ultimate marker of health prevent him from addressing his emotional well-being. Past *memories* of being praised for his appearance reinforce a *bias* toward prioritizing looks over inner balance.

Daniel's *fear* of being seen as weak stops him from seeking help for his mental health, while his *assumption* that exercise alone can solve all his problems keep him from exploring other areas of wellness. Motivated by societal expectations, he *expects* that physical fitness will lead to happiness, but he remains unfulfilled. These subconscious influences prevent Daniel from achieving true holistic health.

ROOT CAUSE

The root of this problem lies in defining fitness too narrowly. True wellness encompasses physical, mental, and emotional health. Focusing solely on the physical aspect limits your ability to live a balanced, healthy, and fulfilling life.

YOUR SOLUTION

1. **Redefine Fitness:** Include mental, emotional, and spiritual wellness as key aspects of your health journey.
2. **Prioritize Mental Health:** Explore practices like mindfulness, therapy, or journaling to address emotional well-being.
3. **Balance Your Routine:** Incorporate activities that nurture your mind and spirit, such as reading, meditation, or quality time with loved ones.
4. **Listen to Your Body:** Recognize signs of stress or burnout and take steps to recover.
5. **Celebrate Holistic Growth:** Focus on how you feel overall, not just how you look or perform physically.

SCRIPTURE REFERENCE

"Dear friend, I pray that you may enjoy good health and that all may go well with you, even as your soul is getting along well." (3 John 1:2)

This verse highlights the importance of holistic wellness, including both physical and inner health.

CLOSING THOUGHT

Believing fitness is only physical can leave you feeling incomplete and unbalanced. By embracing a broader definition of health that includes mental and emotional well-being, you can achieve a more fulfilling and sustainable state of fitness. What area of your health have you been neglecting, and how can you address it today? Remember, true fitness starts from within.

Problem 37: Fearing Sacrifice Will Cost Too Much Joy

How avoiding discipline limits your long-term health and happiness.

Do you avoid healthy habits because they feel like too much of a sacrifice? Many people resist making changes to their lifestyle, fearing that giving up indulgences will make life less enjoyable. This mindset often leads to short-term gratification at the expense of long-term well-being. The problem isn't the sacrifice—it's how you perceive it.

SUBCONSCIOUS INFLUENCES

Think of Maria, who avoids committing to a healthy eating plan because she doesn't want to give up her favorite comfort foods. Her *beliefs* that healthy living equals deprivation keep her from trying. Past *memories* of unsuccessful diets reinforce a *bias* that change always feels restrictive.

Maria's *fear* of losing the joy she associates with food stops her from exploring balanced options, while her *assumptions* that health and happiness are mutually exclusive prevent her from seeing the benefits of discipline. Motivated by a desire to maintain pleasure, she *expects* that any sacrifice will make her life less fulfilling. These subconscious patterns keep her stuck in unhealthy cycles.

ROOT CAUSE

The root of this problem lies in equating discipline with deprivation. Sacrifices made for your health can bring greater joy and freedom over time. When you shift your focus to the benefits rather than the perceived losses, you can embrace healthier habits with a positive mindset.

SCRIPTURE REFERENCE

"No discipline seems pleasant at the time, but painful. Later on, however, it produces a harvest of righteousness and peace for those who have been trained by it." (Hebrews 12:11) This verse highlights the long-term rewards of discipline and sacrifice.

CLOSING THOUGHT

Fearing that sacrifice will cost too much joy keeps you from experiencing the lasting benefits of a healthier lifestyle. By embracing discipline and focusing on the positive outcomes, you can create habits that support both your well-being and happiness. What small change can you make today to invest in your long-term health? Remember, true joy comes from balance, not excess.

Problem 38: Assuming Healthy Habits Are Inconvenient

How misjudging effort keeps you from a better life.

Do you believe that adopting healthy habits will disrupt your routine or take too much effort? Many people avoid making changes to their lifestyle because they perceive them as inconvenient or time-consuming. This mindset keeps you from discovering how small, consistent actions can lead to significant improvements. The problem isn't the habits—it's your assumptions about them.

SUBCONSCIOUS INFLUENCES

Consider Alex, who skips exercise because he thinks it requires hours at the gym. His **beliefs** that healthy living is only for people with plenty of free time discourage him from starting. Past **memories** of failing to maintain a strict fitness regimen create a **bias** that any effort will eventually be wasted.

Alex's **fear** of disrupting his current routine stops him from exploring realistic options, while his **assumptions** that healthy habits require drastic changes keep him stuck. Motivated by a desire for convenience, he **expects** to sacrifice too much for too little gain. These subconscious patterns prevent him from experiencing the benefits of small, manageable changes.

ROOT CAUSE

The root of this problem lies in overestimating the effort required to establish healthy habits. Many effective changes are simple and require only small adjustments to your current routine. Misjudging the effort keeps you from taking the first steps toward a healthier life.

YOUR SOLUTION

1. **Start Small:** Incorporate simple changes, such as a short daily walk or swapping one unhealthy meal for a healthier option.
2. **Focus on Consistency:** Commit to small, sustainable habits rather than overwhelming changes.
3. **Reevaluate Your Time:** Identify moments in your day that could be repurposed for healthier activities.
4. **Set Realistic Goals:** Define specific, achievable actions to track your progress.
5. **Celebrate the Benefits:** Reflect on how even minor adjustments improve your energy, mood, and overall well-being.

SCRIPTURE REFERENCE

"So whether you eat or drink or whatever you do, do it all for the glory of God." (1 Corinthians 10:31)
This verse encourages mindful, intentional living in all areas of life, including health.

CLOSING THOUGHT

Assuming healthy habits are inconvenient prevents you from experiencing the rewards of a better lifestyle. By starting small and focusing on realistic changes, you can make significant progress without overwhelming your routine. What small adjustment can you make today to improve your health? Remember, meaningful change begins with simple, consistent actions.

Problem 39: Letting Past Failures Define Future Efforts

How clinging to past mistakes prevents you from trying again.

Do you avoid pursuing healthy habits because you've failed to maintain them in the past? Many people let previous setbacks dictate their approach to health and wellness, assuming that failure is a sign they're not capable of success. This mindset traps you in a cycle of inaction and prevents you from realizing your potential. The problem isn't the failure—it's letting it define you.

SUBCONSCIOUS INFLUENCES

Take Emma, who stopped exercising after quitting her gym membership six months ago. Her *beliefs* that she's not disciplined enough to maintain a routine keep her from trying again. Past *memories* of failed diets and skipped workouts create a *bias* that future efforts will end the same way.

Emma's *fear* of repeating her mistakes discourages her from setting new goals, while her *assumptions* that success requires perfection keep her stuck. Motivated by a desire to avoid disappointment, she *expects* to fail before she even begins. These subconscious patterns prevent Emma from giving herself the chance to succeed.

ROOT CAUSE

The root of this problem lies in equating past failures with future outcomes. Mistakes are a natural part of growth, but when you internalize them as evidence of your limitations, you miss the opportunity to learn and improve. Breaking free requires reframing failure as feedback rather than finality.

YOUR SOLUTION

1. **Reframe Failure:** View past mistakes as lessons that can guide your future efforts.
2. **Start Fresh:** Set new, realistic goals without comparing them to past attempts.
3. **Focus on Progress:** Celebrate small achievements rather than fixating on perfection.
4. **Seek Support:** Surround yourself with people who encourage you and hold you accountable.
5. **Keep Trying:** Accept that setbacks are part of the journey and use them as motivation to keep moving forward.

SCRIPTURE REFERENCE

"Brothers and sisters, I do not consider myself yet to have taken hold of it. But one thing I do: Forgetting what is behind and straining toward what is ahead, I press on toward the goal..." (Philippians 3:13-14)
This verse encourages perseverance and a forward-focused mindset, leaving past mistakes behind.

CLOSING THOUGHT

Letting past failures define your future efforts limits your ability to grow and achieve your health goals. By learning from your mistakes and approaching each new attempt with fresh determination, you can build resilience and success. What past failure has been holding you back, and how can you reframe it today? Remember, every step forward is a step closer to your goals.

Problem 40: Motivating Change Through Shame

How self-criticism sabotages your health and well-being.

Do you push yourself to adopt healthy habits by focusing on your flaws or shortcomings? Many people try to motivate change by shaming themselves, believing that harsh criticism will lead to better results. While this approach might produce short-term action, it often creates long-term guilt, self-doubt, and resistance. The problem isn't the desire to improve—it's the use of shame as a motivator.

SUBCONSCIOUS INFLUENCES

Consider Rachel, who constantly berates herself for gaining weight and uses negative self-talk to force herself into dieting. Her *beliefs* that self-criticism is necessary for discipline keep her trapped in a cycle of guilt. Past *memories* of being shamed for her appearance create a *bias* that equates worthiness with physical fitness.

Rachel's *fear* of judgment from others intensifies her self-criticism, while her *assumptions* that she needs to be perfect to be accepted drive her actions. Motivated by insecurity, she *expects* failure and punishes herself preemptively. These subconscious influences make it difficult for Rachel to develop a healthy relationship with herself or her goals.

ROOT CAUSE

The root of this problem lies in associating self-worth with perfection and using shame as a tool for improvement. True growth comes from self-compassion and positive reinforcement, not from tearing yourself down. When shame becomes the motivator, it damages both your confidence and your progress.

YOUR SOLUTION

1. **Replace Shame With Compassion:** Speak to yourself with the kindness and encouragement you'd offer a friend.
2. **Focus on Strengths:** Identify what you're doing well and build on those successes.
3. **Set Positive Goals:** Frame your habits around what you want to gain, not what you want to lose.
4. **Practice Gratitude:** Reflect on what your body can do and the progress you've made, however small.
5. **Seek Encouragement:** Surround yourself with supportive people who uplift you and celebrate your efforts.

SCRIPTURE REFERENCE

"I praise you because I am fearfully and wonderfully made; your works are wonderful, I know that full well." (Psalm 139:14) This verse reminds you of your inherent value and the need to treat yourself with respect and care.

CLOSING THOUGHT

Motivating change through shame undermines your confidence and long-term success. By shifting your focus to self-compassion and positive reinforcement, you can build healthier habits and a stronger sense of self-worth. What area of your life have you been using shame to push for change, and how can you replace it with encouragement today? Remember, true growth starts with love, not criticism.

FAITH AND SPIRITUALITY PROBLEMS

Problem 41: Assuming Faith Must Be Earned

How striving for perfection distances you from God's grace.

Do you feel like you have to prove your worth to God through your actions? Many people believe that faith is something they must earn by being perfect, righteous, or without fault. This mindset often leads to guilt, frustration, and a sense of spiritual inadequacy. The problem isn't your desire to grow closer to God—it's the belief that you have to earn His love.

SUBCONSCIOUS INFLUENCES

Consider Jacob, who avoids prayer and church because he feels unworthy after making mistakes. His *beliefs* that God only accepts those who are sinless stem from harsh religious teachings in his childhood. Past *memories* of being reprimanded for falling short of expectations create a *bias* toward seeing God as distant or critical.

Jacob's *fear* of judgment keeps him from seeking God's presence, while his *assumptions* that he must fix himself before approaching God prevent him from experiencing grace. Motivated by a desire to be "good enough," he *expects* failure and withdraws instead of drawing closer. These subconscious patterns make faith feel like an unattainable goal rather than a gift.

ROOT CAUSE

The root of this problem lies in misunderstanding God's unconditional love and grace. Faith is not something you earn through perfection—it's a relationship built on trust, forgiveness, and acceptance. Striving to "deserve" God's love often leads to spiritual burnout and a distorted view of His character.

YOUR SOLUTION

1. **Embrace Grace:** Accept that God's love is a gift, not something you have to earn.
2. **Confess and Release:** Share your struggles with God, trusting in His forgiveness and understanding.
3. **Focus on Relationship:** Shift your faith journey from performance to genuine connection with God.
4. **Rely on Scripture:** Meditate on verses that affirm God's grace and unconditional love.
5. **Let Go of Perfection:** Allow yourself to be human and lean on God's strength, not your own.

SCRIPTURE REFERENCE

"For it is by grace you have been saved, through faith— and this is not from yourselves, it is the gift of God—not by works, so that no one can boast." (Ephesians 2:8-9)
This verse underscores that faith is a gift, freely given, and not something you can earn.

CLOSING THOUGHT

Assuming faith must be earned creates unnecessary barriers to experiencing God's love and grace. By letting go of the need for perfection, you can embrace a deeper, more authentic relationship with Him. What area of your life are you trying to "fix" before approaching God, and how can you surrender it to Him today? Remember, God's love is freely given—just as you are.

Problem 42: Fearing Doubts Disqualify Your Belief

How avoiding questions weakens your faith.

Do you avoid exploring doubts about your faith because you fear it means you don't truly believe? Many people see doubts as a sign of weakness or lack of commitment, leading them to suppress their questions. This mindset often creates a shallow faith that feels fragile and disconnected. The problem isn't your doubts—it's your fear of facing them.

SUBCONSCIOUS INFLUENCES

Take Sarah, who struggles with unanswered questions about her faith but refuses to voice them. Her *beliefs* that true believers never doubt stem from early teachings that equated questions with rebellion. Past *memories* of being criticized for questioning authority create a *bias* against seeking clarity.

Sarah's *fear* of being judged or losing her connection with God keeps her silent, while her *assumptions* that doubt is a sign of failure stop her from seeking understanding. Motivated by a desire to appear faithful, she *expects* rejection if she admits her struggles. These subconscious patterns make her faith feel stagnant and unsupported.

ROOT CAUSE

The root of this problem lies in equating doubt with disbelief. In reality, doubt can be a tool for growth, prompting deeper exploration and a stronger foundation of faith. Suppressing questions often leads to spiritual stagnation and disconnection.

YOUR SOLUTION

1. **Acknowledge Your Doubts:** Recognize that questioning is a natural and healthy part of faith.
2. **Seek Answers:** Study scripture, consult trusted spiritual leaders, and explore resources that address your concerns.
3. **Pray Through Your Questions:** Invite God into your doubts, trusting Him to guide your understanding.
4. **Build Community:** Surround yourself with believers who encourage honest conversations about faith.
5. **Focus on Growth:** Use doubt as an opportunity to deepen your relationship with God rather than withdrawing from Him.

SCRIPTURE REFERENCE

"Immediately the boy's father exclaimed, 'I do believe; help me overcome my unbelief!'" (Mark 9:24)
This verse highlights that faith and doubt can coexist, and God welcomes honest prayers for help and clarity.

CLOSING THOUGHT

Fearing that doubts disqualify your belief keeps you from experiencing the fullness of faith. By addressing your questions with openness and trust, you can deepen your relationship with God and strengthen your spiritual foundation. What doubt have you been avoiding, and how can you start seeking answers today? Remember, faith isn't the absence of doubt—it's trusting God through it.

Problem 43: Associating God's Love With Punishment

How misunderstanding God's nature keeps you distant.

Do you feel like God's love is conditional, tied to your actions, or overshadowed by punishment? Many people view God as a strict disciplinarian, believing His love must be earned or that mistakes automatically invite His wrath. This mindset often leads to fear, shame, and a distant relationship with God. The problem isn't God's love—it's how you perceive it.

SUBCONSCIOUS INFLUENCES

Consider Michael, who hesitates to pray after making a mistake because he feels unworthy of forgiveness. His *beliefs* that God is primarily focused on judgment stem from childhood teachings that emphasized punishment over grace. Past *memories* of being harshly reprimanded for his errors reinforce a *bias* that God's love is transactional.

Michael's *fear* of rejection keeps him from seeking God's presence, while his *assumptions* that forgiveness is only granted after perfection prevent him from experiencing grace. Motivated by guilt, he *expects* punishment instead of love, which creates a cycle of avoidance and spiritual disconnection.

ROOT CAUSE

The root of this problem lies in misunderstanding the balance between God's justice and His mercy. God's love is unconditional, and His discipline, when given, is meant to guide and grow, not to condemn. Focusing solely on punishment distorts His nature and limits your ability to fully receive His love.

YOUR SOLUTION

1. **Study God's Character:** Explore scripture to understand His love, grace, and mercy alongside His justice.
2. **Embrace Forgiveness:** Accept that God's forgiveness is freely given through faith, not earned by actions.
3. **Reframe Discipline:** View God's correction as an act of love meant to guide you, not to harm you.
4. **Seek Connection:** Pray openly, trusting that God desires a relationship with you, even in your imperfection.
5. **Replace Fear With Trust:** Shift your focus from avoiding punishment to growing closer to God's heart.

SCRIPTURE REFERENCE

"The Lord is compassionate and gracious, slow to anger, abounding in love." (Psalm 103:8)
This verse highlights God's loving nature, emphasizing His patience and mercy.

CLOSING THOUGHT

Associating God's love with punishment creates unnecessary fear and distance in your relationship with Him. By embracing His grace and understanding His true nature, you can move past shame and into a deeper connection with Him. What fear is keeping you from fully receiving God's love, and how can you let go of it today? Remember, God's love is constant, not conditional.

Problem 44: Relying on Rituals Without Understanding

How focusing on routines over relationship weakens your faith.

Do you prioritize religious rituals without fully understanding their meaning or purpose? Many people go through the motions of faith practices, believing the act itself is enough to bring them closer to God. While rituals can be valuable, relying on them without understanding often leads to emptiness and frustration. The problem isn't the rituals—it's missing their deeper significance.

SUBCONSCIOUS INFLUENCES

Take Emma, who attends church every Sunday but feels no closer to God in her daily life. Her **beliefs** that attendance alone ensures spiritual growth keep her from seeking a deeper connection. Past **memories** of being praised for outward displays of faith create a **bias** toward focusing on actions rather than heart alignment.

Emma's **assumptions** that rituals automatically lead to spiritual growth prevent her from engaging meaningfully, while her **fear** of doing something "wrong" stops her from exploring a more personal faith. Motivated by routine, she **expects** results from her actions alone, leaving her disconnected from the relationship God desires.

ROOT CAUSE

The root of this problem lies in mistaking rituals for the substance of faith. True spiritual growth comes from understanding, intentionality, and relationship with God, not just outward practices. Without aligning your heart with your actions, rituals lose their transformative power.

YOUR SOLUTION

1. **Reflect on Meaning:** Take time to understand the purpose behind your faith practices.
2. **Seek Heart Alignment:** Ensure that your actions reflect your genuine love for God, not just obligation.
3. **Focus on Relationship:** Prioritize personal prayer, study, and connection with God over routine.
4. **Explore Scripture:** Dive deeper into the biblical basis for rituals to uncover their true significance.
5. **Embrace Authenticity:** Practice faith in ways that feel meaningful and sincere to your relationship with God.

SCRIPTURE REFERENCE

"These people honor me with their lips, but their hearts are far from me." (Matthew 15:8)
This verse reminds you that faith is about connection with God, not just outward actions.

CLOSING THOUGHT

Relying on rituals without understanding reduces faith to empty routines, leaving you unfulfilled. By focusing on the relationship behind the actions, you can deepen your connection with God and experience true spiritual growth. What ritual have you been practicing without reflection, and how can you bring it back to its intended purpose today? Remember, faith starts in the heart, not the habit.

Problem 45: Expecting Immediate Answers to Prayer

How impatience weakens your trust in God.

Do you get discouraged when your prayers don't seem to be answered right away? Many people expect instant results from prayer, viewing unanswered requests as signs of neglect or rejection. This mindset often leads to frustration, doubt, and even a weakened faith. The problem isn't the timing—it's your expectations.

SUBCONSCIOUS INFLUENCES

Consider John, who prayed for a promotion at work but gave up on asking God when it didn't happen immediately. His **beliefs** that prayer should yield quick results stem from a transactional view of his relationship with God. Past **memories** of waiting for unanswered prayers create a **bias** that God is distant or unresponsive.

John's **fear** that his prayers are being ignored discourages him from praying persistently, while his **assumptions** that delays mean rejection make him doubt God's care. Motivated by a desire for control, he **expects** instant answers rather than trusting God's timing. These subconscious patterns make prayer feel like an ineffective tool rather than a source of strength and connection.

ROOT CAUSE

The root of this problem lies in misunderstanding the purpose of prayer and the nature of God's timing. Prayer is not about immediate gratification but about aligning your heart with God's will and trusting His plan. Impatience often blinds you to the ways God is working behind the scenes.

SCRIPTURE REFERENCE

"Rejoice in hope, be patient in tribulation, be constant in prayer." (Romans 12:12)
This verse encourages patience and persistence in prayer, trusting that God is at work.

CLOSING THOUGHT

Expecting immediate answers to prayer can lead to unnecessary doubt and frustration. By trusting God's timing and focusing on the relationship prayer fosters, you can experience deeper faith and peace. What prayer have you been impatiently waiting on, and how can you trust God's timing today? Remember, God's answers are always on time, even when they don't match your schedule.

EDUCATION PROBLEMS

Problem 46: Believing Learning Stops After School

How limiting your growth stifles your potential.

Do you think education ends the moment you graduate? Many people believe that once formal schooling is complete, the need for learning diminishes. This mindset often leads to stagnation, missed opportunities, and a failure to adapt to life's challenges. The problem isn't your schooling—it's the belief that learning has an expiration date.

SUBCONSCIOUS INFLUENCES

Consider Laura, who hasn't pursued personal or professional development since earning her degree. Her *beliefs* that education is confined to classrooms keep her from seeking new knowledge. Past *memories* of struggling with exams create a *bias* that learning is stressful or difficult.

Laura's *fear* of failure prevents her from trying new skills, while her *assumptions* that her formal education is sufficient hold her back from growing. Motivated by a desire for comfort, she *expects* that life will remain manageable without ongoing learning. These subconscious influences lead to a fixed mindset, limiting her potential.

ROOT CAUSE

The root of this problem lies in associating education solely with formal institutions. True learning is a lifelong process that extends beyond classrooms, involving curiosity, adaptability, and a willingness to embrace new experiences. Stopping your education stunts your growth and narrows your opportunities.

YOUR SOLUTION

1. **Adopt a Growth Mindset:** Recognize that learning is a lifelong journey, not a one-time achievement.
2. **Explore New Skills:** Identify areas of interest and pursue knowledge through books, online courses, or hands-on experience.
3. **Embrace Curiosity:** Ask questions, seek answers, and remain open to discovering new perspectives.
4. **Invest in Self-Improvement:** Dedicate time to personal and professional development regularly.
5. **Celebrate Learning Moments:** Acknowledge how continuous education enriches your life and opens doors.

SCRIPTURE REFERENCE

"Let the wise hear and increase in learning, and the one who understands obtain guidance." (Proverbs 1:5)
This verse emphasizes the value of ongoing learning and seeking wisdom throughout life.

CLOSING THOUGHT

Believing learning stops after school limits your ability to grow and adapt. By embracing lifelong education, you can unlock new opportunities and achieve your fullest potential. What's one area where you've stopped learning, and how can you reignite your curiosity today? Remember, growth thrives on continuous discovery.

Problem 47: Fearing Failure Prevents Trying New Skills

How avoiding mistakes keeps you from growth.

Do you hold back from learning new skills because you're afraid of failing? Many people avoid trying unfamiliar things, fearing the embarrassment or frustration that comes with making mistakes. This mindset not only limits your personal growth but also keeps you from discovering untapped potential. The problem isn't the failure—it's your fear of it.

SUBCONSCIOUS INFLUENCES

Take Adam, who has always wanted to learn a musical instrument but avoids starting because he worries about being bad at it. His **beliefs** that failure defines his worth discourage him from taking risks. Past **memories** of being criticized for mistakes create a **bias** that trying something new will lead to judgment.

Adam's **fear** of looking incompetent stops him from even attempting, while his **assumptions** that success should come easily prevent him from embracing the learning process. Motivated by perfectionism, he **expects** instant results, and when they don't come, he gives up. These subconscious patterns leave Adam stuck in his comfort zone, missing opportunities for joy and achievement.

ROOT CAUSE

The root of this problem lies in equating failure with inadequacy rather than growth. Mistakes are an essential part of mastering new skills, and fear of failure often prevents you from realizing how much you can achieve with persistence and patience.

SCRIPTURE REFERENCE

"For the Spirit God gave us does not make us timid, but gives us power, love, and self-discipline." (2 Timothy 1:7) This verse reminds you to approach challenges with courage and persistence, trusting God's strength within you.

CLOSING THOUGHT

Fearing failure prevents you from exploring your potential and experiencing the joy of learning. By embracing mistakes as part of the process, you can grow in confidence and skill. What skill have you been avoiding because of fear, and how can you take the first step today? Remember, growth begins where fear ends.

Problem 48: Assuming Intelligence Is Fixed, Not Grown

How limiting beliefs about ability block your potential.

Do you believe your intelligence or abilities are set in stone? Many people assume that they're either naturally "good" or "bad" at certain things, which discourages them from trying to learn or improve in areas where they struggle. This mindset not only stunts personal development but also keeps you from achieving more. The problem isn't your capacity—it's your belief about it.

SUBCONSCIOUS INFLUENCES

Consider Rachel, who avoids taking on challenging projects at work because she doubts her ability to succeed. Her *beliefs* that intelligence is innate stem from years of hearing phrases like "you're just not a math person." Past *memories* of struggling in certain subjects reinforce a *bias* that she's incapable of improvement.

Rachel's *fear* of failure stops her from trying new things, while her *assumptions* that effort won't make a difference keep her from even starting. Motivated by a desire to protect her self-esteem, she *expects* to fail before she begins. These subconscious influences lock Rachel into a fixed mindset, limiting her ability to grow and succeed.

ROOT CAUSE

The root of this problem lies in adopting a fixed mindset rather than a growth mindset. Intelligence and skills are not static—they can be developed through effort, practice, and persistence. Assuming your abilities are unchangeable prevents you from realizing your full potential.

YOUR SOLUTION

1. **Adopt a Growth Mindset:** Recognize that intelligence and skills can grow with effort and time.
2. **Reframe Challenges:** View difficulties as opportunities to learn rather than evidence of limitations.
3. **Celebrate Effort:** Focus on the process of learning rather than just the outcome.
4. **Seek Feedback:** Use constructive criticism as a tool for growth, not a measure of failure.
5. **Practice Consistently:** Dedicate time to improving skills, knowing progress takes time.

SCRIPTURE REFERENCE

"Do not conform to the pattern of this world, but be transformed by the renewing of your mind." (Romans 12:2)
This verse reminds you that growth and transformation are possible through intentional effort and mindset changes.

CLOSING THOUGHT

Assuming intelligence is fixed limits your ability to learn and grow. By embracing a mindset that values effort and persistence, you can unlock new possibilities and expand your potential. What belief about your abilities has been holding you back, and how can you challenge it today? Remember, growth is always possible with the right mindset.

Problem 49: Associating Asking Questions With Weakness

How avoiding curiosity hinders your growth.

Do you hesitate to ask questions because you fear it will make you look uninformed or incapable? Many people associate seeking clarification or knowledge with weakness, which prevents them from learning and improving. This mindset not only limits your understanding but also keeps you from building meaningful connections with others. The problem isn't the questions—it's your fear of asking them.

SUBCONSCIOUS INFLUENCES

Consider James, who often stays silent in meetings because he doesn't want to seem unprepared. His *beliefs* that asking questions signals incompetence stem from early experiences where he was ridiculed for not knowing the answer. Past *memories* of being embarrassed create a *bias* against seeking help or clarification.

James's *fear* of judgment stops him from engaging, while his *assumptions* that others view him as incapable discourage him from speaking up. Motivated by a desire to protect his image, he *expects* to lose credibility if he asks for clarification. These subconscious influences prevent James from fully participating and growing.

ROOT CAUSE

The root of this problem lies in misunderstanding the value of curiosity. Asking questions is not a sign of weakness—it's a powerful tool for growth and connection. Avoiding questions keeps you stuck in self-doubt and limits your ability to gain new insights or solve problems effectively.

SCRIPTURE REFERENCE

"If any of you lacks wisdom, you should ask God, who gives generously to all without finding fault, and it will be given to you." (James 1:5)
This verse encourages seeking knowledge and wisdom without fear of judgment.

CLOSING THOUGHT

Associating asking questions with weakness limits your ability to grow and connect. By embracing curiosity and valuing the insights questions bring, you can unlock new opportunities for understanding and success. What question have you been holding back, and how can asking it move you forward today? Remember, true strength lies in the pursuit of knowledge.

Problem 50: Motivating Study Only Through Rewards

How external incentives limit your learning potential.

Do you find it hard to focus on learning unless there's a tangible reward at the end? Many people rely on external motivators like grades, recognition, or financial gain to drive their study habits. While rewards can be helpful, relying on them exclusively often undermines intrinsic motivation and the joy of learning. The problem isn't the rewards—it's making them your only reason to learn.

SUBCONSCIOUS INFLUENCES

Take Hannah, who feels unmotivated to learn new skills unless there's a direct payoff, such as a promotion or praise. Her **beliefs** that effort must always lead to immediate rewards stem from childhood experiences of being incentivized with treats for completing homework. Past **memories** of being rewarded for grades but not for effort reinforce a **bias** that learning isn't valuable on its own.

Hannah's **fear** of wasting time keeps her from pursuing knowledge without an obvious benefit, while her **assumptions** that rewards are necessary for effort limit her intrinsic motivation. Motivated by external validation, she **expects** learning to feel unimportant without tangible outcomes. These subconscious patterns hinder her ability to enjoy the process of growth.

ROOT CAUSE

The root of this problem lies in prioritizing external rewards over internal satisfaction. Learning driven by curiosity and personal growth is more fulfilling and sustainable than learning solely for external incentives. Over-reliance on rewards can make education feel like a chore rather than an opportunity.

YOUR SOLUTION

1. **Cultivate Curiosity:** Focus on learning for the sake of growth and discovery, not just for rewards.
2. **Set Personal Goals:** Identify intrinsic motivators, such as mastering a skill or deepening your understanding of a topic.
3. **Celebrate Effort:** Acknowledge progress and the process of learning, even without immediate outcomes.
4. **Balance Rewards and Passion:** Use rewards sparingly and supplement them with goals that excite you personally.
5. **Reframe Success:** Define success as what you learn, not what you earn or achieve externally.

SCRIPTURE REFERENCE

"Set your minds on things above, not on earthly things."
(Colossians 3:2)
This verse encourages focusing on deeper, intrinsic values rather than external, temporary rewards.

CLOSING THOUGHT

Motivating study only through rewards limits your ability to embrace learning as a lifelong, fulfilling process. By shifting your focus to intrinsic goals and personal growth, you can reignite your passion for discovery. What learning goal can you pursue today for its own sake, not for a reward? Remember, the best rewards are the ones that transform you from within.

TIME MANAGEMENT PROBLEMS

Problem 51: Believing Busyness Equals Productivity

How confusing activity with achievement wastes your time.

Do you equate being busy with being productive? Many people fill their schedules with tasks, thinking that constant activity proves their efficiency or worth. However, focusing on busyness often leads to burnout and missed opportunities for meaningful progress. The problem isn't your ambition—it's mistaking busyness for true productivity.

SUBCONSCIOUS INFLUENCES

Consider Alex, who feels accomplished only when his calendar is packed with meetings and deadlines. His *beliefs* that busyness reflects success stem from societal norms that glorify hustle culture. Past *memories* of being praised for working long hours create a *bias* toward prioritizing quantity over quality.

Alex's *fear* of being seen as lazy drives him to overcommit, while his *assumptions* that more work equals more value prevent him from focusing on what truly matters. Motivated by the desire for recognition, he *expects* busyness to lead to success, but often finds himself overwhelmed and unfulfilled. These subconscious patterns keep Alex stuck in a cycle of inefficiency.

ROOT CAUSE

The root of this problem lies in valuing activity over results. Productivity isn't about doing more—it's about doing what matters most. Confusing the two leads to wasted time, unnecessary stress, and missed opportunities for meaningful impact.

YOUR SOLUTION

1. **Prioritize Tasks:** Focus on high-value activities that align with your goals and eliminate unnecessary tasks.
2. **Plan Strategically:** Use tools like time blocking or the Eisenhower Matrix to structure your day around priorities.
3. **Take Breaks:** Recognize that rest and reflection are essential for maintaining energy and focus.
4. **Measure Results:** Evaluate success by what you achieve, not how much you do.
5. **Learn to Say No:** Protect your time by declining commitments that don't serve your goals or well-being.

SCRIPTURE REFERENCE

"Be very careful, then, how you live—not as unwise but as wise, making the most of every opportunity." (Ephesians 5:15-16)

This verse reminds you to use your time wisely and focus on what truly matters.

CLOSING THOUGHT

Believing busyness equals productivity keeps you trapped in a cycle of constant activity without meaningful progress. By prioritizing what matters most and letting go of unnecessary tasks, you can achieve more with less stress. What task can you eliminate today to focus on what truly counts? Remember, productivity is about purpose, not just motion.

Problem 52: Fearing Prioritization Will Displease Others

How avoiding focus to please everyone wastes your time.

Do you avoid prioritizing your tasks because you're afraid of disappointing others? Many people overextend themselves, trying to say "yes" to every request in an effort to maintain harmony or meet others' expectations. This mindset often leads to overwhelm, inefficiency, and neglect of your own goals. The problem isn't your willingness to help—it's your fear of prioritizing what matters most.

SUBCONSCIOUS INFLUENCES

Think about Mia, who frequently puts her own deadlines on hold to assist coworkers with their projects. Her *beliefs* that helping others is more important than her own work come from cultural and familial expectations to always be accommodating. Past *memories* of being praised for selflessness create a *bias* toward putting others first.

Mia's *fear* of being perceived as selfish prevents her from setting boundaries, while her *assumptions* that others will resent her if she prioritizes her own work keep her overcommitted. Motivated by a desire for approval, she *expects* that saying no will damage relationships, leaving her stressed and falling behind on her goals.

ROOT CAUSE

The root of this problem lies in misunderstanding the balance between helping others and protecting your priorities. Prioritization isn't selfish—it's essential for achieving meaningful results and maintaining your well-being. Avoiding it leads to burnout and resentment, ultimately harming both you and those you aim to help.

YOUR SOLUTION

1. **Set Clear Boundaries:** Communicate your availability and limits to others while remaining respectful.
2. **Prioritize Your Goals:** Identify your most important tasks and focus on them first.
3. **Learn to Say No:** Decline requests that don't align with your priorities or values.
4. **Offer Alternatives:** When you can't help, suggest other resources or solutions to support the person asking.
5. **Reframe Self-Care:** Understand that prioritizing your goals allows you to serve others more effectively in the long term.

SCRIPTURE REFERENCE

"It is not good to have zeal without knowledge, nor to be hasty and miss the way." (Proverbs 19:2)
This verse encourages thoughtful action, reminding you to focus on what is wise and necessary rather than rushing to please everyone.

CLOSING THOUGHT

Fearing prioritization will displease others keeps you trapped in a cycle of overcommitment and stress. By setting boundaries and focusing on what truly matters, you can achieve your goals while supporting others in a healthier, more sustainable way. What task or request can you say "no" to today to prioritize your well-being? Remember, effective focus benefits everyone in the end.

Problem 53: Assuming Procrastination Is Harmless

How delaying tasks sabotages your success.

Do you put off important tasks, assuming you'll have time to handle them later? Many people believe procrastination is harmless, often underestimating the stress, missed opportunities, and compromised results it creates. The problem isn't the delay—it's the mindset that justifies it.

SUBCONSCIOUS INFLUENCES

Take Daniel, who frequently waits until the last minute to complete work projects. His **beliefs** that he performs better under pressure reinforce his procrastination habit. Past **memories** of pulling off successful last-minute efforts create a **bias** that procrastination isn't a real problem.

Daniel's **fear** of starting difficult tasks makes procrastination feel like a relief, while his **assumptions** that there's always enough time to catch up keep him from prioritizing effectively. Motivated by avoidance, he **expects** his future self to handle the stress, often compromising the quality of his work and creating unnecessary anxiety.

ROOT CAUSE

The root of this problem lies in underestimating the cumulative effects of procrastination. Delaying tasks doesn't just affect deadlines—it chips away at your focus, energy, and long-term goals. Overcoming procrastination requires shifting from avoidance to accountability.

1. **Recognize the Cost:** Reflect on how procrastination impacts your stress, productivity, and outcomes.
2. **Break Tasks Into Steps:** Tackle large projects by dividing them into manageable actions to reduce overwhelm.
3. **Set Immediate Deadlines:** Create short-term goals to maintain urgency and momentum.
4. **Reward Progress:** Celebrate small achievements to stay motivated as you complete tasks.
5. **Reflect on Long-Term Goals:** Remind yourself of how timely action aligns with your bigger objectives.

SCRIPTURE REFERENCE

"Whoever watches the wind will not plant; whoever looks at the clouds will not reap." (Ecclesiastes 11:4)
This verse highlights the danger of waiting for the perfect moment, encouraging immediate and intentional action.

CLOSING THOUGHT

Assuming procrastination is harmless undermines your success and increases unnecessary stress. By addressing tasks promptly and breaking them into manageable steps, you can regain control of your time and achieve better results. What important task have you been putting off, and how can you take the first step today? Remember, success begins with action.

Problem 54: Allowing Distractions to Replace Discipline

How losing focus derails your progress.

Do you let minor distractions interrupt your priorities, thinking you'll return to your tasks later? Many people underestimate how distractions, such as social media, entertainment, or unnecessary errands, steal their time and energy. This mindset often leads to decreased productivity and unmet goals. The problem isn't the distractions—it's allowing them to replace discipline.

SUBCONSCIOUS INFLUENCES

Consider Sarah, who frequently scrolls through her phone during work breaks but struggles to refocus afterward. Her *beliefs* that taking frequent breaks helps productivity encourage her habits. Past *memories* of procrastinating without immediate consequences create a *bias* that distractions aren't a real problem.

Sarah's *fear* of missing out on social updates keeps her glued to her phone, while her *assumptions* that she can "make up time later" prevent her from setting boundaries. Motivated by instant gratification, she *expects* small distractions to have minimal impact, but they often derail her focus and momentum.

ROOT CAUSE

The root of this problem lies in prioritizing immediate satisfaction over long-term goals. Distractions, when unmanaged, undermine your ability to concentrate and execute effectively. Replacing distractions with discipline requires intentionality and awareness of their impact.

YOUR SOLUTION

1. **Identify Your Distractions:** Take note of the habits or activities that pull you away from your priorities.
2. **Set Clear Boundaries:** Limit your access to distractions during work or focus time, such as turning off notifications.
3. **Use Focus Strategies:** Implement techniques like the Pomodoro method or time blocking to stay disciplined.
4. **Reflect on Goals:** Keep your bigger objectives in mind to resist the pull of temporary diversions.
5. **Reward Discipline:** Celebrate completed tasks as a way to reinforce focus and commitment.

SCRIPTURE REFERENCE

"**Let your eyes look straight ahead; fix your gaze directly before you." (Proverbs 4:25)**
This verse emphasizes the importance of staying focused on your path without being swayed by distractions.

CLOSING THOUGHT

Allowing distractions to replace discipline hinders your progress and wastes valuable time. By managing interruptions and maintaining focus, you can accomplish more and achieve your goals with confidence. What distraction is stealing your attention, and how can you eliminate it today? Remember, discipline drives success.

Problem 55: Expecting Deadlines to Create Motivation

How relying on urgency weakens your commitment.

Do you wait for deadlines to spur you into action, believing the pressure will boost your productivity? Many people procrastinate, expecting that looming deadlines will naturally provide the focus and motivation they need. While this might work in the short term, it often leads to stress, poor-quality work, and a lack of sustainable habits. The problem isn't the deadlines—it's relying on them as your primary motivator.

SUBCONSCIOUS INFLUENCES

Consider Mike, who delays starting important projects until the last possible moment. His *beliefs* that he works better under pressure keep him from planning effectively. Past *memories* of successfully pulling off last-minute efforts reinforce a *bias* that deadlines are the only way to ensure productivity.

Mike's *fear* of wasting time on non-urgent tasks stops him from beginning early, while his *assumptions* that deadlines will "save" him allow him to neglect preparation. Motivated by the adrenaline of urgency, he *expects* to thrive under pressure but often delivers rushed and subpar results. These subconscious patterns hinder his ability to create consistent and disciplined work habits.

ROOT CAUSE

The root of this problem lies in relying on external pressure rather than internal motivation. Deadlines can drive short-term results, but they often compromise long-term growth and the quality of your efforts. True productivity comes from developing habits that sustain focus and progress over time.

SCRIPTURE REFERENCE

"The plans of the diligent lead to profit as surely as haste leads to poverty." (Proverbs 21:5)

This verse reminds you of the value of steady, intentional work over rushed efforts.

CLOSING THOUGHT

Expecting deadlines to create motivation limits your ability to achieve consistent, high-quality results. By developing proactive habits and focusing on progress over urgency, you can reduce stress and work more effectively. What task are you waiting until the last minute to start, and how can you take the first step today? Remember, motivation grows through discipline, not deadlines.

COMMUNICATION PROBLEMS

Problem 56: Assuming Others Understand Your Intentions

How miscommunication creates unnecessary conflict.

Do you assume that your actions or words are clear to others without explaining them? Many people believe their intentions are obvious, but this often leads to misunderstandings, hurt feelings, or unmet expectations. The problem isn't your intentions—it's assuming they don't need to be communicated.

SUBCONSCIOUS INFLUENCES

Consider Anna, who gets frustrated when her coworkers don't follow through on tasks she delegates. Her *beliefs* that people "should know better" come from her own high standards for understanding instructions. Past *memories* of being misunderstood create a *bias* that communication is futile or unnecessary.

Anna's *fear* of over-explaining makes her avoid clarifying details, while her *assumptions* that her coworkers think the way she does lead to incomplete communication. Motivated by a desire to seem efficient, she *expects* others to automatically grasp her intentions, resulting in frustration and conflict.

ROOT CAUSE

The root of this problem lies in overestimating how well others can interpret your thoughts or actions. Clear and intentional communication is essential for building trust, resolving conflicts, and achieving goals. Assuming understanding leads to missed opportunities for connection and progress.

1. **Clarify Your Intentions:** Clearly articulate your thoughts, feelings, and expectations to avoid misunderstandings.
2. **Seek Feedback:** Ask others to repeat or summarize your instructions to ensure clarity.
3. **Practice Empathy:** Recognize that others may interpret your actions differently based on their own perspectives.
4. **Be Open to Questions:** Encourage dialogue to clarify uncertainties and strengthen mutual understanding.
5. **Reflect on Outcomes:** Learn from past miscommunications to improve your future interactions.

SCRIPTURE REFERENCE

"Let your conversation be always full of grace, seasoned with salt, so that you may know how to answer everyone." (Colossians 4:6)
This verse emphasizes the importance of thoughtful, intentional communication.

CLOSING THOUGHT

Assuming others understand your intentions often leads to unnecessary conflict and frustration. By communicating clearly and inviting dialogue, you can build stronger relationships and avoid misunderstandings. What assumption have you made recently, and how can you clarify it today? Remember, connection grows through intentional communication.

Problem 57: Fearing Honesty Will Create Conflict

How avoiding truth weakens your relationships.

Do you hold back from being honest with others because you're afraid it will cause tension or disagreement? Many people avoid expressing their true thoughts or feelings, thinking it's better to keep the peace. However, this fear often leads to unresolved issues, resentment, and strained relationships. The problem isn't your desire for harmony—it's avoiding honesty to maintain it.

SUBCONSCIOUS INFLUENCES

Consider Rachel, who rarely voices her concerns with her partner, even when something bothers her. Her *beliefs* that conflict damages relationships stem from past experiences where arguments led to estrangement. Past *memories* of being criticized for speaking her mind create a *bias* toward staying silent.

Rachel's *fear* of upsetting her partner prevents her from addressing issues, while her *assumptions* that honesty will escalate into conflict keep her disengaged. Motivated by a desire to avoid discomfort, she *expects* her feelings to fade with time, but they often intensify. These subconscious patterns prevent her from building genuine trust and connection.

ROOT CAUSE

The root of this problem lies in misunderstanding the role of honesty in healthy relationships. While conflict may arise, addressing issues with openness and respect fosters deeper understanding and growth. Avoiding truth erodes trust and creates emotional distance over time.

YOUR SOLUTION

1. **Start Small:** Practice honesty in low-stakes situations to build confidence in expressing yourself.
2. **Focus on Delivery:** Use calm, respectful language to share your thoughts without escalating tension.
3. **Address Issues Early:** Speak up before frustrations build into larger conflicts.
4. **Invite Dialogue:** Encourage open communication by asking for the other person's perspective.
5. **Embrace Growth:** Recognize that healthy relationships often grow stronger through honest discussions.

SCRIPTURE REFERENCE

"Therefore each of you must put off falsehood and speak truthfully to your neighbor, for we are all members of one body." (Ephesians 4:25)

This verse highlights the importance of honesty as a foundation for trust and unity.

CLOSING THOUGHT

Fearing honesty will create conflict often leads to unresolved issues and weakened connections. By approaching honesty with care and respect, you can build stronger, more authentic relationships. What truth have you been avoiding, and how can you express it with love today? Remember, honesty is the path to genuine harmony.

Problem 58: Motivating Conversations Through Ego

How prioritizing your own needs disrupts meaningful communication.

Do you approach conversations primarily to prove your point or validate your own perspective? Many people unconsciously use communication as a way to boost their ego, prioritizing being right over building understanding. This mindset often leads to frustration, disconnection, and missed opportunities for meaningful dialogue. The problem isn't the conversation—it's the intention behind it.

SUBCONSCIOUS INFLUENCES

Consider Kevin, who dominates discussions with his friends, always steering the conversation back to his own experiences. His *beliefs* that his insights are more valuable stem from a need for validation. Past *memories* of being overlooked in group settings create a *bias* toward speaking louder or longer to maintain control.

Kevin's *fear* of being ignored drives him to prioritize his opinions over listening, while his *assumptions* that others share his perspective prevent him from truly understanding their views. Motivated by a desire to feel important, he *expects* others to appreciate his input, often leaving them feeling unheard or dismissed.

ROOT CAUSE

The root of this problem lies in prioritizing self-interest over mutual understanding. Conversations thrive on balance, where both parties feel valued and heard. When ego takes center stage, it undermines connection and reduces communication to competition.

YOUR SOLUTION

1. **Shift Your Focus:** Approach conversations with curiosity and a genuine interest in others' perspectives.
2. **Practice Active Listening:** Pay full attention to the speaker without planning your response as they talk.
3. **Balance Contributions:** Ensure you're sharing and listening equally during discussions.
4. **Ask Open-Ended Questions:** Encourage others to share their thoughts, making them feel valued.
5. **Reflect on Intentions:** Before speaking, ask yourself if your input serves the conversation or just your ego.

SCRIPTURE REFERENCE

"Do nothing out of selfish ambition or vain conceit. Rather, in humility value others above yourselves." (Philippians 2:3) This verse reminds you to prioritize humility and mutual respect in your interactions.

CLOSING THOUGHT

Motivating conversations through ego often leads to shallow or strained connections. By focusing on understanding and valuing others, you can foster deeper, more meaningful communication. What conversation can you approach with humility and curiosity today? Remember, true dialogue builds bridges, not barriers.

Problem 59: Associating Silence With Peace

How avoiding communication creates unspoken tension.

Do you assume that staying silent about issues or feelings will maintain peace in your relationships? Many people avoid conversations they find uncomfortable, believing that silence prevents conflict. However, this often leads to unresolved problems, hidden resentment, and emotional distance. The problem isn't the silence—it's assuming it equates to harmony.

SUBCONSCIOUS INFLUENCES

Consider Emily, who never addresses her frustrations with her partner, hoping they will resolve on their own. Her **beliefs** that discussing issues will create unnecessary tension stem from past experiences of heated arguments. Past **memories** of failed attempts to communicate reinforce a **bias** toward avoidance.

Emily's **fear** of confrontation keeps her from expressing her needs, while her **assumptions** that her partner should understand her feelings without her saying anything lead to misunderstandings. Motivated by a desire to keep the peace, she **expects** the relationship to improve over time, but instead, the distance grows. These subconscious patterns erode the trust and connection in her relationship.

ROOT CAUSE

The root of this problem lies in misunderstanding the role of communication in maintaining peace. True harmony comes from addressing issues constructively, not ignoring them. Silence often creates more tension, as unspoken feelings and unmet expectations build over time.

1. **Acknowledge the Tension:** Recognize that silence often signals unresolved issues rather than peace.
2. **Initiate the Conversation:** Approach the topic calmly and respectfully, focusing on solutions instead of blame.
3. **Express Yourself Clearly:** Share your feelings and needs openly without expecting the other person to read your mind.
4. **Encourage Dialogue:** Invite the other person to share their perspective and listen without interruption.
5. **Practice Constructive Conflict:** Learn to address disagreements in ways that strengthen, rather than harm, the relationship.

SCRIPTURE REFERENCE

"Therefore, each of you must put off falsehood and speak truthfully to your neighbor, for we are all members of one body." (Ephesians 4:25)

This verse emphasizes the importance of honesty and open communication in maintaining unity and understanding.

CLOSING THOUGHT

Associating silence with peace often leads to hidden tension and unspoken resentment. By addressing issues openly and constructively, you can foster stronger, more authentic relationships. What concern have you been avoiding, and how can you address it today with grace and clarity? Remember, true peace comes from resolution, not avoidance.

Problem 60: Believing Talking Is the Same as Listening

How dominating conversations prevents genuine connection.

Do you think that expressing your thoughts is enough to build strong communication? Many people believe that talking more automatically strengthens relationships, but they often fail to listen actively. This mindset creates one-sided conversations, leaving others feeling unheard and undervalued. The problem isn't your willingness to share—it's assuming that talking is all it takes.

SUBCONSCIOUS INFLUENCES

Take Mark, who often interrupts others during discussions to share his own experiences. His *beliefs* that his input is always valuable stem from a desire to feel relevant and respected. Past *memories* of being praised for his insights reinforce a *bias* that speaking more equates to contributing more.

Mark's *fear* of not being heard drives him to dominate conversations, while his *assumptions* that others naturally feel included prevent him from noticing their disengagement. Motivated by a need for validation, he *expects* others to appreciate his input without considering their feelings. These subconscious influences weaken his relationships and create emotional distance.

ROOT CAUSE

The root of this problem lies in confusing talking with connecting. Genuine communication requires active listening, empathy, and a balance between speaking and hearing. Without listening, conversations become self-centered and fail to build meaningful connections.

YOUR SOLUTION

1. **Pause and Listen:** Practice fully hearing the other person before forming your response.
2. **Ask Questions:** Show interest in others' perspectives by asking thoughtful, open-ended questions.
3. **Reflect on Their Words:** Summarize or acknowledge what the other person has shared to show understanding.
4. **Balance Contributions:** Ensure conversations involve equal input from all parties.
5. **Focus on Connection:** Shift your goal from expressing yourself to fostering mutual understanding.

SCRIPTURE REFERENCE

"My dear brothers and sisters, take note of this: Everyone should be quick to listen, slow to speak, and slow to become angry." (James 1:19)
This verse emphasizes the importance of listening as a foundation for meaningful communication.

CLOSING THOUGHT

Believing talking is the same as listening prevents you from building genuine connections. By prioritizing active listening and fostering balanced conversations, you can strengthen relationships and create deeper understanding. What conversation can you approach today with a listening ear instead of a speaking agenda? Remember, listening is the key to connection.

LEADERSHIP PROBLEMS

Problem 61: Fearing Team Success Will Diminish Your Role

How insecurity prevents effective leadership.

Do you feel threatened when your team members shine, worrying that their success will overshadow your contributions? Many leaders struggle with insecurity, fearing that empowering others will diminish their own value. This mindset often leads to micromanagement, distrust, and missed opportunities for growth. The problem isn't your leadership—it's your fear of losing control.

SUBCONSCIOUS INFLUENCES

Consider Jessica, a manager who hesitates to delegate important tasks because she fears her team members might outperform her. Her *beliefs* that her worth is tied to her individual achievements prevent her from celebrating the success of others. Past *memories* of being overlooked for promotions reinforce a *bias* toward self-preservation over collaboration.

Jessica's *fear* of losing recognition drives her to micromanage, while her *assumptions* that her team might replace her keep her from building trust. Motivated by a need to protect her status, she *expects* failure when she relinquishes control, creating a toxic work environment. These subconscious patterns stifle both her growth and her team's potential.

ROOT CAUSE

The root of this problem lies in misunderstanding leadership as a solitary endeavor rather than a collaborative process. True leadership is about empowering others to succeed, which ultimately reflects positively on the entire team, including the leader.

YOUR SOLUTION

1. **Redefine Success:** Recognize that your role as a leader is to guide and support, not to compete with your team.
2. **Delegate Strategically:** Assign tasks that align with your team members' strengths and trust them to deliver.
3. **Celebrate Contributions:** Acknowledge and reward your team's achievements without feeling threatened.
4. **Build Trust:** Foster an environment of collaboration where everyone's growth benefits the group.
5. **Focus on Long-Term Impact:** Understand that empowering others strengthens your legacy as a leader.

SCRIPTURE REFERENCE

"Each of you should use whatever gift you have received to serve others, as faithful stewards of God's grace in its various forms." (1 Peter 4:10)
This verse reminds you that leadership is about serving and stewarding others' talents for the greater good.

CLOSING THOUGHT

Fearing team success will diminish your role prevents you from becoming an effective and inspiring leader. By empowering and celebrating others, you can create a thriving team and leave a lasting impact. What task can you delegate today to demonstrate trust in your team? Remember, a leader's greatness lies in the success of those they lead.

Problem 62: Assuming Authority Means Isolation

How believing leadership requires distance weakens your influence.

Do you feel the need to separate yourself from your team to maintain authority? Many leaders mistakenly assume that building strong connections with their team will undermine their position. This mindset often leads to loneliness, distrust, and a lack of collaboration. The problem isn't your authority—it's isolating yourself to protect it.

SUBCONSCIOUS INFLUENCES

Take David, a department head who avoids socializing with his team because he fears they won't respect him if he gets too close. His *beliefs* that authority requires distance come from observing strict hierarchies in previous workplaces. Past *memories* of leaders who were criticized for being "too friendly" reinforce a *bias* toward keeping relationships strictly professional.

David's *fear* of losing respect stops him from engaging personally, while his *assumptions* that familiarity breeds contempt prevent him from building trust. Motivated by a desire to maintain control, he *expects* his team to respect his authority without personal connection, leading to disengagement and inefficiency.

ROOT CAUSE

The root of this problem lies in misunderstanding the balance between authority and approachability. Leadership is not about isolating yourself; it's about creating an environment of trust and collaboration where your authority inspires respect through genuine connection.

1. **Redefine Authority:** Understand that leadership is strengthened by trust, not distance.
2. **Engage Personally:** Show genuine interest in your team members' lives and well-being.
3. **Build Collaborative Relationships:** Foster open dialogue and mutual respect without compromising your role.
4. **Model Approachability:** Be available to your team for guidance, feedback, and support.
5. **Balance Connection and Boundaries:** Maintain professionalism while being personable and empathetic.

SCRIPTURE REFERENCE

"Be shepherds of God's flock that is under your care, watching over them—not because you must, but because you are willing, as God wants you to be; not pursuing dishonest gain, but eager to serve." (1 Peter 5:2)

This verse emphasizes servant leadership, where care and connection strengthen authority.

CLOSING THOUGHT

Assuming authority means isolation weakens your ability to lead effectively. By building trust and fostering meaningful relationships with your team, you can create a more collaborative and productive environment. What step can you take today to connect with someone you lead? Remember, strong leadership bridges gaps—it doesn't create them.

Problem 63: Associating Leadership With Control

How micromanaging stifles growth and creativity.

Do you equate strong leadership with having full control over every detail? Many leaders struggle with relinquishing authority, believing that tight oversight ensures success. However, micromanagement often discourages creativity, undermines trust, and reduces team morale. The problem isn't your leadership—it's associating it with excessive control.

SUBCONSCIOUS INFLUENCES

Consider Sarah, who reviews every team member's work before it's finalized, often redoing tasks herself. Her *beliefs* that a leader must ensure perfection prevent her from delegating effectively. Past *memories* of being blamed for mistakes reinforce a *bias* toward maintaining strict control.

Sarah's *fear* of losing credibility drives her to overmanage, while her *assumptions* that her team can't meet her standards lead to mistrust. Motivated by a desire to avoid failure, she *expects* to carry the burden alone, which creates frustration for herself and her team. These subconscious patterns limit her team's growth and innovation.

ROOT CAUSE

The root of this problem lies in misunderstanding leadership as control rather than empowerment. True leadership involves trusting others to take ownership of their work while providing guidance and support. Over-controlling leadership stifles creativity, productivity, and team development.

SCRIPTURE REFERENCE

"Where there is no guidance, a people falls, but in an abundance of counselors there is safety." (Proverbs 11:14) This verse highlights the value of collaboration and shared responsibility in leadership.

CLOSING THOUGHT

Associating leadership with control limits your team's potential and creates unnecessary stress. By trusting and empowering others, you can inspire growth, innovation, and success. What task can you delegate today to demonstrate trust in your team? Remember, great leaders guide—they don't micromanage.

Problem 64: Avoiding Accountability to Save Face

How avoiding responsibility undermines trust and growth.

Do you avoid taking responsibility for your mistakes to protect your image? Many people fear that admitting fault will damage their reputation or authority, so they deflect blame or hide their errors. However, avoiding accountability can create mistrust, hinder personal growth, and weaken relationships. The problem isn't your mistakes—it's your fear of facing them.

SUBCONSCIOUS INFLUENCES

Think about Tom, a team leader who never admits when his strategy fails. His *beliefs* that vulnerability will make him appear weak prevent him from taking responsibility. Past *memories* of being punished for mistakes in his career create a *bias* against showing imperfection.

Tom's *fear* of losing credibility stops him from acknowledging his errors, while his *assumptions* that others will judge him harshly keep him from owning up to his mistakes. Motivated by the desire to maintain control, he *expects* to protect his reputation by deflecting blame, but this damages trust and teamwork. These subconscious patterns prevent him from learning from his mistakes and growing as a leader.

ROOT CAUSE

The root of this problem lies in misunderstanding accountability as weakness. Admitting mistakes is a powerful tool for learning, growth, and strengthening relationships. Avoiding accountability not only hinders progress but also creates a culture of blame and defensiveness.

1. **Acknowledge Mistakes Quickly:** Own up to errors as soon as they happen, demonstrating humility and integrity.
2. **Learn from Feedback:** Use constructive criticism as a tool for growth and improvement.
3. **Apologize When Necessary:** Take responsibility for the impact of your actions on others and seek to make things right.
4. **Foster Transparency:** Create an environment where accountability is valued and seen as a strength.
5. **Embrace Imperfection:** Recognize that mistakes are part of the process and an opportunity for growth.

SCRIPTURE REFERENCE

"Whoever conceals their sins does not prosper, but the one who confesses and renounces them finds mercy." (Proverbs 28:13)

This verse emphasizes the importance of acknowledging our mistakes and seeking forgiveness for true growth and peace.

CLOSING THOUGHT

Avoiding accountability to save face only diminishes your credibility and creates barriers to progress. By taking responsibility for your actions, you strengthen trust and demonstrate the courage to grow. What mistake can you own today to move forward with integrity? Remember, accountability is a sign of strength, not weakness.

Problem 65: Expecting Loyalty Without Trust

How demanding loyalty without building trust damages relationships.

Do you expect others to remain loyal to you without showing them trust and respect? Many people believe that loyalty should be automatic, but without trust, loyalty becomes difficult to maintain. This mindset can create resentment, tension, and disconnection. The problem isn't your desire for loyalty—it's the assumption that it can exist without the foundation of trust.

SUBCONSCIOUS INFLUENCES

Consider James, who feels frustrated when his colleagues don't stand by him during tough situations. His *beliefs* that loyalty is earned by position or authority prevent him from building authentic trust. Past *memories* of being let down by others reinforce a *bias* that loyalty should be unconditional.

James's *fear* of being vulnerable makes him hesitant to open up or trust others, while his *assumptions* that loyalty should come first lead to unspoken expectations. Motivated by a desire to be supported, he *expects* loyalty from his team, but without demonstrating trustworthiness, he finds his relationships weakening. These subconscious patterns make it hard to foster the strong, trusting connections necessary for true loyalty.

ROOT CAUSE

The root of this problem lies in misunderstanding loyalty as something that can exist in isolation. Trust is the foundation for loyalty, and without it, relationships are fragile. Expecting loyalty without showing trust only creates frustration and distance.

SCRIPTURE REFERENCE

"The one who has unreliable friends soon comes to ruin, but there is a friend who sticks closer than a brother."
(Proverbs 18:24)
This verse highlights the value of true friendships built on trust and loyalty.

CLOSING THOUGHT

Expecting loyalty without trust damages relationships and creates unmet expectations. By focusing on building trust and demonstrating integrity, you can cultivate loyalty that lasts. How can you show more trust in those around you today to strengthen your connections? Remember, loyalty grows where trust is planted.

SELF-WORTH PROBLEMS

Problem 66: Associating Accomplishments With Value

How tying your worth to achievements undermines your self-esteem.

Do you measure your worth by your achievements and accomplishments? Many people believe that their value is determined by how much they accomplish, whether it's at work, in relationships, or in personal pursuits. This mindset often leads to burnout, self-doubt, and a constant need for external validation. The problem isn't your desire for success—it's connecting your worth to your accomplishments.

SUBCONSCIOUS INFLUENCES

Consider Laura, who constantly feels inadequate unless she's achieving something. Her *beliefs* that she must prove her value through accomplishments stem from messages she received growing up that praised performance over who she was. Past *memories* of receiving love and recognition only for achievements reinforce a *bias* that success equals worth.

Laura's *fear* of being seen as unimportant drives her to overachieve, while her *assumptions* that others won't value her without tangible results leave her feeling empty when she doesn't succeed. Motivated by a desire for approval, she *expects* validation through her accomplishments but often feels unfulfilled. These subconscious patterns prevent Laura from experiencing true self-worth and satisfaction.

ROOT CAUSE

The root of this problem lies in equating personal value with external achievements. While success is important, it should not define who you are. When your worth is tied to what you do, it's easy to fall into a cycle of constant striving, leaving you feeling exhausted and unworthy when you fall short.

YOUR SOLUTION

1. **Redefine Value:** Understand that your worth is inherent and not based on what you accomplish.
2. **Practice Self-Compassion:** Treat yourself with kindness and understanding, regardless of your success or failure.
3. **Celebrate Being, Not Doing:** Focus on personal growth, relationships, and well-being as measures of success.
4. **Limit Comparisons:** Stop measuring yourself against others' accomplishments and focus on your unique journey.
5. **Reflect on Strengths:** Regularly remind yourself of your qualities and attributes that make you valuable, beyond what you achieve.

SCRIPTURE REFERENCE

"For we are God's handiwork, created in Christ Jesus to do good works, which God prepared in advance for us to do." (Ephesians 2:10)
This verse reminds you that your worth comes from being created by God, not from what you accomplish.

CLOSING THOUGHT

Associating accomplishments with your value limits your ability to experience true fulfillment and self-love. By recognizing your inherent worth and focusing on inner growth, you can find peace and satisfaction regardless of external success. What is one way you can affirm your worth today, without relying on achievement? Remember, you are valuable simply because you exist.

Problem 67: Fearing Criticism Defines Who You Are

How fear of judgment prevents personal growth.

Do you avoid new challenges or shy away from feedback because you fear criticism will define you? Many people associate being criticized with failure, believing that it reflects their abilities or personal worth. This mindset often leads to avoidance of constructive feedback and missed opportunities for growth. The problem isn't the criticism—it's how you allow it to impact your self-perception.

SUBCONSCIOUS INFLUENCES

Take Rachel, who avoids taking on leadership roles at work because she fears negative feedback. Her **beliefs** that criticism is a personal attack come from past experiences where feedback was harsh or judgmental. Past **memories** of being judged for mistakes reinforce a **bias** that any criticism means she is inadequate.

Rachel's **fear** of being seen as incompetent prevents her from stepping out of her comfort zone, while her **assumptions** that criticism defines her value keep her from embracing growth. Motivated by a desire to protect her self-esteem, she **expects** to fail when she is criticized, avoiding challenges and feedback. These subconscious patterns prevent Rachel from reaching her full potential.

ROOT CAUSE

The root of this problem lies in misinterpreting criticism as an attack on your identity rather than an opportunity for improvement. Criticism, when received constructively, can be a valuable tool for growth. Fear of criticism often stems from a lack of self-acceptance and a desire for perfection, both of which prevent personal development.

YOUR SOLUTION

1. **Reframe Criticism:** View feedback as a tool for growth, not a reflection of your worth.
2. **Embrace Vulnerability:** Recognize that receiving criticism shows strength and willingness to improve.
3. **Focus on Growth:** Focus on how feedback can help you become better, rather than on the fear of judgment.
4. **Separate Feedback From Identity:** Understand that criticism is about your actions or work, not about who you are as a person.
5. **Seek Constructive Feedback:** Encourage others to provide helpful, actionable feedback that supports your development.

SCRIPTURE REFERENCE

"The Lord reproves those he loves, as a father the son he delights in." (Proverbs 3:12)
This verse reminds you that correction and criticism, when given with love, are meant to guide you toward growth and improvement.

CLOSING THOUGHT

Fearing criticism as a reflection of your worth limits your ability to grow and learn. By accepting feedback as a gift, you can transform it into a powerful tool for self-improvement. What recent criticism have you feared, and how can you use it to grow today? Remember, your value is not determined by what others say—it's rooted in who you are.

Problem 68: Believing Perfection Is Necessary for Love

How striving for perfection hinders authentic connections.

Do you think you need to be perfect in order to be loved? Many people believe that only when they meet a certain standard of success or flawlessness can they truly be worthy of love and affection. This mindset often leads to insecurity, anxiety, and the fear of being rejected. The problem isn't your desire to be loved—it's thinking you have to be perfect to deserve it.

SUBCONSCIOUS INFLUENCES

Consider Mark, who constantly overachieves and hides his vulnerabilities in his relationships. His *beliefs* that love must be earned through perfection stem from past experiences where he was only praised when he succeeded. Past *memories* of conditional love, where approval was given only when he excelled, create a *bias* that love is tied to perfection.

Mark's *fear* of being seen as imperfect keeps him from showing his true self, while his *assumptions* that he must always meet expectations prevent him from experiencing authentic love. Motivated by a desire to feel accepted, he *expects* rejection when he isn't perfect, and as a result, he isolates himself emotionally. These subconscious patterns prevent Mark from forming deep, unconditional connections.

ROOT CAUSE

The root of this problem lies in misunderstanding love as something conditional rather than unconditional. Love doesn't require perfection—true love is accepting someone for who they are, flaws and all. When you tie your worth to perfection, you block the possibility of real, lasting connections.

YOUR SOLUTION

1. **Embrace Imperfection:** Accept that you don't have to be perfect to be loved or worthy of affection.
2. **Build Self-Acceptance:** Learn to love yourself for who you are, not just for what you accomplish or how you look.
3. **Be Vulnerable:** Show your true self to others, allowing them to love you for the real you, flaws and all.
4. **Practice Compassion:** Recognize that everyone has imperfections, and those imperfections make us human and relatable.
5. **Reframe Love:** Understand that love is about connection, not perfection.

SCRIPTURE REFERENCE

"But God demonstrates his own love for us in this: While we were still sinners, Christ died for us." (Romans 5:8)
This verse underscores that love is given unconditionally, not based on perfection or behavior.

CLOSING THOUGHT

Believing that perfection is necessary for love keeps you from experiencing the authentic connections you deserve. By embracing your imperfections and practicing self-love, you open yourself to deeper, more genuine relationships. What imperfection can you embrace today to show yourself love? Remember, love thrives in authenticity, not perfection.

Problem 69: Assuming Flaws Make You Unworthy

How focusing on imperfections undermines your self-worth.

Do you believe that your flaws make you unworthy of love or success? Many people struggle with feelings of inadequacy, believing that their imperfections define their value. This mindset often leads to low self-esteem, self-doubt, and an inability to embrace opportunities. The problem isn't your flaws—it's how you perceive them.

SUBCONSCIOUS INFLUENCES

Think about Julia, who constantly compares herself to others and feels unworthy when she falls short. Her *beliefs* that her flaws make her less deserving of love or success come from childhood experiences where mistakes were met with criticism. Past *memories* of being judged for her imperfections create a *bias* toward seeing them as personal failures.

Julia's *fear* of being rejected keeps her from fully embracing opportunities, while her *assumptions* that others won't accept her flaws prevent her from being authentic. Motivated by a desire to be "perfect," she *expects* rejection and failure when she shows her imperfections. These subconscious patterns limit Julia's ability to grow and pursue her true potential.

ROOT CAUSE

The root of this problem lies in tying your worth to your flaws rather than embracing your humanity. Everyone has flaws, and they don't diminish your value or potential. Believing your flaws make you unworthy prevents you from experiencing the love, success, and joy that come from accepting yourself as you are.

YOUR SOLUTION

1. **Embrace Your Imperfections:** Accept that your flaws are part of what makes you uniquely valuable.
2. **Practice Self-Compassion:** Treat yourself with the same kindness and understanding you offer to others.
3. **Reframe Mistakes:** View mistakes as opportunities for growth rather than proof of inadequacy.
4. **Focus on Strengths:** Recognize your strengths and build on them, instead of solely focusing on perceived flaws.
5. **Seek Support:** Surround yourself with people who appreciate you for who you are, flaws and all.

SCRIPTURE REFERENCE

"I praise you because I am fearfully and wonderfully made; your works are wonderful, I know that full well." (Psalm 139:14)

This verse reminds you that you are wonderfully made, and your worth is inherent, not defined by imperfections.

CLOSING THOUGHT

Assuming your flaws make you unworthy blocks your ability to see your true value. By embracing your imperfections and treating yourself with compassion, you can unlock your full potential. What flaw have you been focusing on, and how can you embrace it today? Remember, your value comes from who you are, not from being perfect.

Problem 70: Letting Comparisons Shape Your Confidence

How comparing yourself to others erodes your self-worth.

Do you measure your worth by comparing yourself to others? Many people fall into the trap of constantly comparing their lives, achievements, and appearances to those around them. This mindset often leads to feelings of inadequacy, jealousy, and a constant need for validation. The problem isn't the comparisons—it's allowing them to define your sense of self-worth.

SUBCONSCIOUS INFLUENCES

Consider Brian, who feels insecure about his career progress because he constantly compares himself to his more successful peers. His **beliefs** that success should look the same for everyone prevent him from appreciating his unique path. Past **memories** of being praised for achievements rather than for who he is reinforce a **bias** toward external validation.

Brian's **fear** of not measuring up drives him to constantly compare his progress to others, while his **assumptions** that others are more accomplished lead him to feel inadequate. Motivated by a desire for approval, he **expects** to feel inferior unless he matches others' successes. These subconscious patterns make it hard for Brian to celebrate his own accomplishments.

ROOT CAUSE

The root of this problem lies in misunderstanding success and self-worth as being externally determined. When you constantly compare yourself to others, you lose sight of your unique value and journey. True confidence comes from within, not from measuring yourself against others.

YOUR SOLUTION

1. **Recognize Your Value:** Understand that your worth is not determined by others' achievements or appearance.
2. **Focus on Your Journey:** Celebrate your personal progress and the unique path you're on, rather than comparing it to someone else's.
3. **Limit Social Comparisons:** Reduce the time you spend comparing yourself to others, especially on social media.
4. **Practice Gratitude:** Reflect on your accomplishments and the blessings you have, focusing on what makes you unique.
5. **Build Self-Acceptance:** Learn to love yourself as you are, without needing external validation.

SCRIPTURE REFERENCE

"Do not compare yourself with others. Each person is unique in the eyes of God." (Galatians 6:4)
This verse reminds you that you are uniquely created and shouldn't measure your worth against others.

CLOSING THOUGHT

Letting comparisons shape your confidence prevents you from embracing your unique journey and potential. By focusing on your own growth and appreciating your individuality, you can build true self-worth. What comparison has been affecting your confidence, and how can you shift your focus today? Remember, your worth comes from who you are, not who you compare yourself to.

CONFLICT RESOLUTION PROBLEMS

Problem 71: Believing Apologies Equal Weakness

How avoiding accountability harms relationships.

Do you avoid apologizing, fearing that it will make you appear weak or inferior? Many people struggle with admitting their mistakes, thinking that apologizing diminishes their strength or authority. However, this mindset often leads to unresolved conflict, strained relationships, and personal growth setbacks. The problem isn't the apology—it's your fear of vulnerability and what it represents.

SUBCONSCIOUS INFLUENCES

Consider Brian, who often avoids apologizing to his friends or colleagues, even when he's in the wrong. His **beliefs** that apologizing means admitting weakness come from past experiences where apologies were seen as signs of failure. Past **memories** of being criticized or punished after apologizing reinforce a **bias** that humility equals defeat.

Brian's **fear** of losing respect prevents him from acknowledging his mistakes, while his **assumptions** that others will view him as weak or less competent discourage him from owning up. Motivated by a desire to maintain his image, he **expects** that apologizing will diminish his authority or value, which only creates distance and tension in his relationships.

ROOT CAUSE

The root of this problem lies in misunderstanding the power of humility and accountability. Apologizing is not a sign of weakness; it is a demonstration of strength, maturity, and a commitment to growth. Avoiding apologies harms both your relationships and your ability to develop personally.

YOUR SOLUTION

1. **Reframe Apologies:** Recognize that apologizing is a strength, not a weakness. It shows integrity and maturity.
2. **Acknowledge Your Mistakes:** Be willing to admit when you're wrong and take responsibility for your actions.
3. **Practice Humility:** Understand that apologizing doesn't diminish your worth—it demonstrates respect for others.
4. **Seek Resolution:** Apologizing paves the way for healing, restoring trust and connection in relationships.
5. **Learn from Mistakes:** Use apologies as an opportunity to grow and prevent future misunderstandings.

SCRIPTURE REFERENCE

"Therefore, if you are offering your gift at the altar and there remember that your brother or sister has something against you, leave your gift there in front of the altar. First go and be reconciled to them; then come and offer your gift." **(Matthew 5:23-24)**

This verse highlights the importance of reconciliation and humility in maintaining healthy relationships.

CLOSING THOUGHT

Believing that apologies equal weakness limits your ability to grow and repair relationships. By embracing humility and accountability, you can strengthen your connections and become a more authentic and respected person. What situation can you approach with humility today and offer a sincere apology? Remember, true strength lies in the courage to acknowledge your mistakes and learn from them.

Problem 72: Assuming Anger Solves Problems

How letting anger control your reactions leads to unnecessary conflict.

Do you often react with anger when faced with frustration or challenges? Many people assume that expressing anger will force others to listen or change, but in reality, it often leads to more problems. Anger, when unchecked, clouds judgment, creates conflict, and damages relationships. The problem isn't your emotions—it's letting anger dictate your responses.

SUBCONSCIOUS INFLUENCES

Consider Mark, who tends to raise his voice when things don't go his way at work. His **beliefs** that anger commands attention stem from childhood experiences where loud voices were used to assert control. Past **memories** of being praised for standing up for himself with anger reinforce a **bias** that it's the best way to get results.

Mark's **fear** of being ignored or dismissed pushes him to escalate situations with anger, while his **assumptions** that others will respect him more when he's forceful prevent him from seeking peaceful solutions. Motivated by a need to be heard, he **expects** that anger will make his point clear, but it often alienates those around him. These subconscious patterns prevent Mark from resolving issues constructively.

ROOT CAUSE

The root of this problem lies in misunderstanding the true power of communication and conflict resolution. Anger, when expressed inappropriately, only amplifies tension and blocks resolution. Effective problem-solving requires patience, understanding, and calm communication, not an emotional outburst.

YOUR SOLUTION

1. **Pause Before Reacting:** Take a moment to calm down and think before responding in anger.
2. **Use "I" Statements:** Express your feelings without blaming others to avoid escalation.
3. **Seek Understanding:** Focus on understanding the other person's perspective rather than asserting your own.
4. **Manage Emotions:** Practice techniques such as deep breathing or mindfulness to control your reactions.
5. **Focus on Solutions:** Shift your energy from anger to problem-solving, focusing on what can be done to resolve the issue.

SCRIPTURE REFERENCE

"Everyone should be quick to listen, slow to speak and slow to become angry, because human anger does not produce the righteousness that God desires." (James 1:19-20)
This verse encourages restraint in anger, reminding you that it is not a productive emotion in conflict resolution.

CLOSING THOUGHT

Assuming anger solves problems often leads to more conflict and frustration. By managing your emotions and seeking peaceful solutions, you can create healthier, more productive relationships. What situation can you approach with calmness and patience today? Remember, true strength lies in controlling your anger, not letting it control you.

Problem 73: Fearing Compromise Means Defeat

How avoiding compromise limits growth and progress.

Do you avoid compromise because you believe it means you're giving up or losing? Many people think that compromise is a sign of weakness or failure, leading them to hold tightly to their own opinions or desires. This mindset can cause unnecessary conflict and prevent collaboration. The problem isn't the compromise—it's the fear of what it represents.

SUBCONSCIOUS INFLUENCES

Consider Olivia, who refuses to adjust her plans in group projects, convinced that giving in would make her look inferior. Her *beliefs* that compromise is the same as losing stem from past experiences where giving in felt like admitting defeat. Past *memories* of being pressured into compromises that didn't feel fair create a *bias* that all compromise leads to personal loss.

Olivia's *fear* of losing control drives her to resist any suggestion that doesn't align with her own view, while her *assumptions* that she must always stand her ground prevent her from finding mutual ground. Motivated by a need to appear strong, she *expects* compromise to undermine her, leading to a rigid mindset and a breakdown in cooperation. These subconscious patterns prevent Olivia from seeing the benefits of flexibility and mutual benefit.

ROOT CAUSE

The root of this problem lies in equating compromise with weakness or submission. In reality, compromise is a powerful tool for collaboration, progress, and growth. Fear of compromise often arises from insecurity, a lack of trust, or the mistaken belief that compromising on a small issue means you've lost on a larger one.

YOUR SOLUTION

1. **Reframe Compromise:** Understand that compromise is a strength, not a defeat. It fosters cooperation and mutual respect.
2. **Focus on Win-Win Solutions:** Look for solutions that benefit everyone, not just yourself.
3. **Practice Flexibility:** Recognize that being open to other ideas can lead to better outcomes for all involved.
4. **Communicate Your Needs:** Be clear about your priorities, and listen to others' priorities as well.
5. **Let Go of Perfection:** Understand that compromise doesn't mean settling for less; it's about working together to find the best solution.

SCRIPTURE REFERENCE

"Let us therefore make every effort to do what leads to peace and to mutual edification." (Romans 14:19)
This verse encourages collaboration and finding peaceful solutions through mutual understanding, emphasizing the importance of compromise in relationships.

CLOSING THOUGHT

Fearing compromise leads to unnecessary conflict and missed opportunities for collaboration. By seeing compromise as a tool for growth and unity, you can find solutions that work for everyone. What situation in your life requires compromise, and how can you approach it with an open mind today? Remember, compromise isn't a loss—it's a path to progress.

Problem 74: Allowing Assumptions to Replace Communication

How jumping to conclusions creates unnecessary misunderstandings.

Do you often assume you know what others are thinking or feeling without asking them? Many people make assumptions about situations or others' intentions, believing they understand without truly clarifying. This mindset leads to misunderstandings, conflict, and missed opportunities for deeper connection. The problem isn't the assumption—it's not taking the time to communicate effectively.

SUBCONSCIOUS INFLUENCES

Consider John, who assumes his friend is upset with him after a brief, vague text message. His **beliefs** that people only reach out when something is wrong cause him to jump to conclusions. Past **memories** of similar situations where misunderstandings led to arguments reinforce a **bias** that silence means conflict.

John's **fear** of rejection prevents him from asking for clarity, while his **assumptions** that his friend is angry prevent him from reaching out. Motivated by insecurity, he **expects** that the situation is negative, leading to unnecessary tension. These subconscious patterns create barriers to effective communication and trust.

ROOT CAUSE

The root of this problem lies in assuming you know what others are thinking or feeling without taking the time to communicate. Assumptions often come from past experiences, fears, or biases that cloud judgment. They prevent genuine connection and often lead to more confusion and conflict.

SCRIPTURE REFERENCE

"Do not judge by appearances, but judge with right judgment." (John 7:24)

This verse emphasizes the importance of understanding and seeking clarity before making conclusions or judgments about others.

CLOSING THOUGHT

Allowing assumptions to replace communication creates unnecessary misunderstandings and conflict. By taking the time to clarify and communicate openly, you can build stronger, more trusting relationships. What assumptions have you made recently that need to be addressed, and how can you approach them with open communication today? Remember, understanding comes from listening, not assuming.

Problem 75: Motivating Action Through Retaliation

How revenge-driven motivations harm your progress and relationships.

Do you sometimes find yourself taking action out of a desire to "get back" at someone or prove a point? Many people are driven by the need to retaliate when they feel wronged, but this motivation often leads to more harm than good. Instead of resolving issues, it creates more conflict, stress, and negative energy. The problem isn't standing up for yourself—it's using revenge as the driving force for action.

SUBCONSCIOUS INFLUENCES

Consider Sarah, who decides to work extra hard to outdo a colleague who was rude to her in a meeting. Her *beliefs* that revenge is a valid response to unfair treatment stem from past experiences where standing up for herself felt empowering. Past *memories* of situations where taking revenge gave her a sense of justice reinforce a *bias* toward retaliatory behavior.

Sarah's *fear* of feeling powerless pushes her to take revenge, while her *assumptions* that showing strength through retaliation will make her feel validated prevent her from seeking peaceful resolutions. Motivated by a desire to "right the wrong," she *expects* her actions to bring closure, but instead, she feels more stressed and disconnected. These subconscious patterns prevent Sarah from fostering long-term, healthy solutions.

ROOT CAUSE

The root of this problem lies in believing that retaliation will lead to satisfaction or resolution. In reality, revenge only prolongs conflict and strengthens negative emotions. Instead of fostering peace, it deepens division and prevents personal growth or healing.

YOUR SOLUTION

1. **Shift Your Focus:** Instead of reacting out of revenge, focus on positive, constructive actions that align with your values.
2. **Seek Understanding:** Approach conflicts with the goal of understanding the other person's perspective, rather than proving your point.
3. **Release the Need for Revenge:** Recognize that revenge only adds to the pain and that letting go of anger promotes healing.
4. **Respond with Integrity:** Take action that reflects your values and character, not your desire to retaliate.
5. **Forgive and Move On:** Understand that forgiveness doesn't mean condoning the wrong, but freeing yourself from the burden of resentment.

SCRIPTURE REFERENCE

"Do not take revenge, my dear friends, but leave room for God's wrath, for it is written: 'It is mine to avenge; I will repay,' says the Lord." (Romans 12:19)
This verse emphasizes the importance of trusting in God's justice and letting go of the need for personal vengeance.

CLOSING THOUGHT

Motivating action through retaliation creates more harm and keeps you trapped in negative cycles. By focusing on healthy, constructive responses, you can foster peace, growth, and stronger relationships. What conflict in your life could benefit from forgiveness instead of retaliation? Remember, true strength lies in letting go of the need for revenge and choosing peace instead.

COMMUNITY AND SOCIAL IMPACT PROBLEMS

Problem 76: Assuming One Person Can't Make a Difference

How underestimating your impact prevents positive change.

Do you ever feel that your actions or efforts won't make a difference because you're just one person? Many people feel powerless in the face of larger issues, thinking that their individual contributions won't matter. This mindset prevents you from taking action, and by doing so, it keeps you from creating the change you desire. The problem isn't your influence—it's believing it's too small to matter.

SUBCONSCIOUS INFLUENCES

Take David, who wants to volunteer in his community but doubts his ability to make a significant impact. His **beliefs** that change requires large-scale action stem from societal messages that emphasize collective power over individual effort. Past **memories** of feeling overlooked or insignificant reinforce a **bias** that his efforts won't be noticed or valued.

David's **fear** of failure and being dismissed keeps him from acting, while his **assumptions** that real change only happens through major initiatives prevent him from starting small. Motivated by a desire to be impactful, he **expects** his contributions to fall short, leading to inaction. These subconscious patterns prevent David from realizing the power of small, consistent efforts.

ROOT CAUSE

The root of this problem lies in misunderstanding the power of individual action. While large movements are important, every significant change starts with individual actions. Believing that one person can't make a difference limits your ability to contribute to the greater good.

YOUR SOLUTION

1. **Recognize Your Influence:** Understand that every action, no matter how small, contributes to larger change.
2. **Start Small:** Begin with manageable goals and actions, knowing that they can grow and lead to greater impact over time.
3. **Focus on Consistency:** Consistency is key to creating lasting change. Small, repeated efforts make a significant difference in the long run.
4. **Lead by Example:** Your actions can inspire others to take similar steps, multiplying your impact.
5. **Celebrate Every Step:** Acknowledge even the smallest progress, as every contribution adds up to something bigger.

SCRIPTURE REFERENCE

"Do not despise these small beginnings, for the Lord rejoices to see the work begin." (Zechariah 4:10)
This verse reminds you that small actions are significant in God's eyes and can lead to great things.

CLOSING THOUGHT

Assuming one person can't make a difference limits your potential to create change. By starting small and remaining consistent, you can have a profound impact on your community and beyond. What change can you start making today, no matter how small? Remember, every great movement begins with one person taking action.

Problem 77: Fearing Judgment for Speaking Out

How silence in the face of injustice keeps you stuck.

Do you hold back from speaking your truth because you fear judgment or criticism? Many people avoid addressing difficult issues or standing up for what they believe in because they worry about how others will perceive them. This fear of judgment often leads to silence, which perpetuates injustice and prevents progress. The problem isn't speaking out—it's allowing fear to silence you.

SUBCONSCIOUS INFLUENCES

Consider Amanda, who witnesses unfair treatment at her workplace but chooses not to speak up because she's afraid of being labeled as troublemaker. Her *beliefs* that speaking out will lead to negative consequences stem from past experiences where voicing concerns resulted in conflict or rejection. Past *memories* of being criticized for taking a stand reinforce a *bias* toward staying silent.

Amanda's *fear* of judgment keeps her from addressing the issue, while her *assumptions* that speaking out will harm her reputation prevent her from taking action. Motivated by a desire to fit in and avoid conflict, she *expects* rejection or backlash if she challenges the status quo. These subconscious patterns prevent Amanda from using her voice to create positive change.

ROOT CAUSE

The root of this problem lies in misunderstanding the role of courage and integrity. Fear of judgment can paralyze you, but speaking out in the face of injustice is an act of courage that can inspire others to do the same. Suppressing your voice to avoid criticism only perpetuates silence and allows injustice to persist.

YOUR SOLUTION

1. **Recognize Your Value:** Understand that your voice is powerful and worthy of being heard, even in the face of judgment.
2. **Focus on Integrity:** Speak out because it aligns with your values, not because of how others will respond.
3. **Prepare for Backlash:** Accept that speaking out might lead to criticism, but remember that it can also inspire others and promote change.
4. **Seek Support:** Find allies who share your beliefs and can help amplify your voice.
5. **Practice Courage:** Begin by speaking out in smaller situations, and build your confidence to address larger challenges.

SCRIPTURE REFERENCE

"Do not be afraid of them; the Lord your God himself will fight for you." (Deuteronomy 3:22)
This verse reminds you that God supports you in speaking out for justice, giving you the courage to stand firm in your beliefs.

CLOSING THOUGHT

Fearing judgment for speaking out keeps you from creating positive change. By choosing to use your voice, you can inspire others and help bring about transformation. What injustice have you been avoiding speaking up about, and how can you address it today with courage? Remember, silence often enables the problem, but speaking out brings the possibility of change.

Problem 78: Letting Biases Shape Group Dynamics

How unchecked biases create division and hinder collaboration.

Do you find yourself favoring certain people or ideas over others because of preconceived notions or biases? Many people unknowingly allow their biases to influence how they interact with others, which can lead to exclusion, misunderstandings, and missed opportunities for collaboration. The problem isn't having preferences—it's letting those biases limit your ability to work effectively with a diverse group.

SUBCONSCIOUS INFLUENCES

Take Maria, who tends to promote ideas from colleagues she feels are more similar to her, while dismissing contributions from others. Her *beliefs* that people like her are more competent stem from past experiences where she was surrounded by similar individuals. Past *memories* of being part of a homogeneous group create a *bias* toward ideas and people who align with her background.

Maria's *fear* of conflict or discomfort prevents her from considering perspectives that differ from her own, while her *assumptions* that people from different backgrounds may not "get it" stop her from engaging fully. Motivated by the desire for harmony and efficiency, she *expects* others to align with her ideas, but this limits creativity and collaboration. These subconscious patterns hinder Maria's ability to tap into the full potential of her team.

ROOT CAUSE

The root of this problem lies in allowing unconscious biases to shape interactions and decision-making. Biases are natural, but when they are left unchecked, they prevent fair, open-minded, and

159

inclusive collaboration. The lack of awareness of these biases can lead to missed opportunities for innovation and growth.

> **YOUR SOLUTION**
>
> 1. **Recognize Your Biases:** Acknowledge the biases you may have, whether they are based on appearance, background, or experiences.
> 2. **Challenge Your Assumptions:** Regularly question whether your assumptions about others are fair and based on evidence.
> 3. **Seek Diverse Perspectives:** Actively seek out opinions and ideas from individuals with different backgrounds and experiences.
> 4. **Promote Inclusion:** Encourage open discussions where everyone feels heard and valued, regardless of their background or status.
> 5. **Reflect on Group Dynamics:** Regularly evaluate how group decisions are made and ensure all voices are considered in the process.

SCRIPTURE REFERENCE

"Do not judge by appearances, but judge with right judgment." (John 7:24)

This verse reminds you to look beyond surface-level judgments and make decisions based on fairness and truth.

CLOSING THOUGHT

Letting biases shape group dynamics limits your ability to collaborate effectively and creates division. By recognizing your biases and striving for inclusion, you can foster stronger, more innovative teams. What bias might you be unconsciously allowing to shape your interactions, and how can you challenge it today? Remember, diversity of thought and experience is key to creating meaningful progress.

Problem 79: Believing Change Happens Without Effort

How expecting change to occur naturally leads to stagnation.

Do you believe that change will happen on its own, without needing much effort or intention? Many people want transformation in their lives but expect it to come effortlessly or passively. This mindset can lead to disappointment and inaction, as real change requires consistent effort, discipline, and focus. The problem isn't the desire for change—it's the belief that it will happen without active involvement.

SUBCONSCIOUS INFLUENCES

Consider James, who dreams of getting in shape but waits for motivation to hit him rather than making a plan. His *beliefs* that change will happen when the timing is right prevent him from taking action now. Past *memories* of attempting change only when he felt inspired create a *bias* that effort isn't needed until he feels "ready."

James's *fear* of failure and discomfort stops him from getting started, while his *assumptions* that change will come naturally keep him from committing to the hard work required. Motivated by a desire for an easy fix, he *expects* change to occur with minimal effort, but that expectation only leads to frustration. These subconscious patterns prevent James from achieving the results he desires.

ROOT CAUSE

The root of this problem lies in misunderstanding the process of change. True transformation requires consistent effort and the willingness to face discomfort and challenges. Believing that change happens without effort leads to procrastination and missed opportunities.

SCRIPTURE REFERENCE

"Do not be deceived: God cannot be mocked. A man reaps what he sows." (Galatians 6:7)
This verse emphasizes that lasting change requires active effort, and the results are based on the actions you take.

CLOSING THOUGHT

Believing that change happens without effort prevents you from taking the necessary steps to achieve transformation. By committing to consistent action and embracing the process, you can create the change you desire. What change have you been waiting for to happen on its own, and how can you start working toward it today? Remember, change is not a passive process—it's the result of intentional action.

Problem 80: Avoiding Collaboration Due to Distrust

How suspicion blocks teamwork and progress.

Do you hesitate to collaborate with others because you don't fully trust them? Many people hold back from working together, fearing that others will not fulfill their responsibilities or that their ideas will be stolen. This mindset prevents growth, creates isolation, and limits collective success. The problem isn't working with others—it's the distrust that undermines collaboration.

SUBCONSCIOUS INFLUENCES

Take Tim, who often prefers to work alone because he doubts his colleagues' abilities to contribute effectively. His *beliefs* that others will not do their part stem from past experiences of being let down by teammates. Past *memories* of failed collaborations reinforce a *bias* that others cannot be trusted.

Tim's *fear* of being taken advantage of prevents him from delegating, while his *assumptions* that others will drop the ball make him hesitant to ask for help. Motivated by a desire for control and a lack of trust, he *expects* others to fail, causing him to isolate himself and limit his team's potential. These subconscious patterns prevent Tim from tapping into the power of collaboration.

ROOT CAUSE

The root of this problem lies in letting past experiences or fear of betrayal affect your ability to trust others in the present. While collaboration requires trust and openness, the fear of being let down often creates barriers to effective teamwork. When you avoid collaboration due to distrust, you rob yourself of opportunities for growth and shared success.

1. **Challenge Your Assumptions:** Recognize that not everyone will act the same way as those who have disappointed you in the past.
2. **Build Trust Gradually:** Start with smaller tasks and increase responsibility as trust is built over time.
3. **Communicate Clearly:** Ensure expectations are understood and agreed upon by all parties involved.
4. **Foster Openness:** Encourage transparency and honesty in your collaborative efforts to minimize misunderstandings.
5. **Embrace Shared Success:** Recognize that working together can lead to better results than working alone, and the collective effort creates a sense of accomplishment for everyone involved.

SCRIPTURE REFERENCE

"Two are better than one, because they have a good return for their labor." (Ecclesiastes 4:9)
This verse emphasizes the value of collaboration, highlighting the benefits of working together in unity.

CLOSING THOUGHT

Avoiding collaboration due to distrust limits your ability to grow and achieve greater success. By fostering trust, open communication, and shared responsibility, you can unlock the power of teamwork. What collaboration have you been avoiding because of distrust, and how can you take the first step toward building trust today? Remember, teamwork thrives on trust and mutual respect.

DECISION-MAKING PROBLEMS

Problem 81: Fearing Responsibility for Outcomes

How avoiding accountability undermines your leadership.

Do you avoid taking on responsibility because you're afraid of the consequences if things don't go as planned? Many people shy away from stepping up because they fear failure or blame. This mindset prevents you from seizing opportunities for growth and leadership. The problem isn't responsibility—it's the fear of what comes with it.

SUBCONSCIOUS INFLUENCES

Consider Emily, who always tries to pass off decision-making to others, fearing that if things go wrong, she'll be blamed. Her *beliefs* that responsibility equals failure come from past experiences where she was criticized for things outside her control. Past *memories* of failure and rejection reinforce a *bias* toward avoiding situations where she might be blamed.

Emily's *fear* of criticism or judgment makes her reluctant to step up, while her *assumptions* that failure will reflect badly on her prevent her from embracing leadership opportunities. Motivated by a desire to avoid negative outcomes, she *expects* to fail if she takes responsibility, which leads to inaction and missed growth. These subconscious patterns prevent Emily from becoming the leader she could be.

ROOT CAUSE

The root of this problem lies in misunderstanding the relationship between responsibility and growth. Responsibility is a key part of leadership and success, and though it comes with risks, it also provides opportunities for personal growth and accomplishment. Fearing responsibility for outcomes prevents you from embracing challenges and seizing the benefits of taking charge.

YOUR SOLUTION

1. **Reframe Responsibility:** Understand that taking responsibility is a chance to grow, not a risk to avoid.
2. **Embrace Ownership:** Acknowledge that both successes and failures are part of the learning process.
3. **Develop Resilience:** See failure as a stepping stone to success rather than something to fear or avoid.
4. **Take Initiative:** Step up when needed, even if the outcome is uncertain, and focus on what can be learned from the process.
5. **Seek Support:** If you feel overwhelmed, find a mentor or support system to help guide you through challenges.

SCRIPTURE REFERENCE

"Commit to the Lord whatever you do, and he will establish your plans." (Proverbs 16:3)
This verse encourages you to take responsibility and trust that God will guide your efforts, even when outcomes are uncertain.

CLOSING THOUGHT

Fearing responsibility for outcomes limits your potential and growth. By embracing accountability and seeing it as a chance to learn and lead, you can unlock new opportunities for success. What responsibility have you been avoiding, and how can you step up today with confidence? Remember, true leadership comes from embracing responsibility, not avoiding it.

Problem 82: Associating Risks With Recklessness

How avoiding calculated risks keeps you from achieving your potential.

Do you avoid taking risks because you fear they will lead to failure or disaster? Many people equate risk-taking with recklessness, believing that any risk is dangerous and should be avoided. This mindset can prevent growth, innovation, and the pursuit of new opportunities. The problem isn't taking risks—it's misunderstanding the difference between reckless and calculated risks.

SUBCONSCIOUS INFLUENCES

Take Daniel, who stays in a job he doesn't enjoy because he's afraid of the financial risk that comes with changing careers. His **beliefs** that risk is always risky stem from past experiences where taking chances led to negative outcomes. Past **memories** of losses or failures reinforce a **bias** that risks are to be avoided at all costs.

Daniel's **fear** of failure prevents him from making bold decisions, while his **assumptions** that risks always lead to bad outcomes keep him in a state of inaction. Motivated by the desire for security, he **expects** that playing it safe will protect him from loss, but it also limits his potential for growth. These subconscious patterns keep him stuck in a cycle of stagnation.

ROOT CAUSE

The root of this problem lies in misunderstanding risk as inherently harmful. While reckless decisions can lead to disaster, calculated risks—those taken with careful planning and foresight—can open the door to new possibilities, success, and fulfillment. Fear of risk often stems from a lack of confidence or a fixed mindset about safety.

YOUR SOLUTION

1. **Reframe Risk:** Understand that taking risks doesn't mean acting recklessly; it means stepping out of your comfort zone with a plan.
2. **Calculate Your Risks:** Evaluate the potential benefits and consequences of a decision before jumping in.
3. **Start Small:** Begin with manageable risks and gradually build your confidence as you see the results of your efforts.
4. **Trust Yourself:** Believe in your ability to make informed decisions and handle the outcomes, whether positive or negative.
5. **Learn from Every Experience:** See each risk as an opportunity to grow, regardless of the outcome.

SCRIPTURE REFERENCE

"Whoever is careful about the word of God is wise, and whoever is careful about what they do will receive understanding." (Proverbs 2:11)
This verse reminds you that wisdom comes from making thoughtful, calculated decisions, not avoiding them out of fear.

CLOSING THOUGHT

Associating risks with recklessness keeps you from taking the necessary steps toward success and growth. By approaching risks with careful thought and planning, you can unlock new opportunities and reach your full potential. What risk have you been avoiding, and how can you take a calculated step toward it today? Remember, calculated risks lead to growth, while avoiding them keeps you stagnant.

Problem 83: Believing Indecision Is Safe

How avoiding decisions keeps you stuck in uncertainty.

Do you struggle with making decisions, thinking that avoiding them is the safest choice? Many people fear making the wrong choice, so they delay decisions or remain indecisive, believing it will keep them from failure or negative outcomes. However, avoiding decisions often leads to missed opportunities, stagnation, and unnecessary stress. The problem isn't the decision—it's the fear of making the wrong one.

SUBCONSCIOUS INFLUENCES

Take Rachel, who constantly delays decisions about her career path because she fears choosing the wrong direction. Her **beliefs** that making the wrong choice will lead to permanent failure come from past experiences where she made mistakes and faced consequences. Past **memories** of situations where decisions led to regret reinforce a **bias** that indecision is safer than making a choice.

Rachel's **fear** of failure and regret keeps her from committing to any path, while her **assumptions** that the perfect decision exists prevent her from seeing that all decisions carry some risk. Motivated by a desire to avoid negative outcomes, she **expects** that indecision will protect her, but it only creates more confusion and missed opportunities.

ROOT CAUSE

The root of this problem lies in misunderstanding indecision as a form of protection. While avoiding decisions may feel safer in the short term, it only leads to further uncertainty and a lack of control over your life. Real growth comes from making decisions and learning from them, not from avoiding them altogether.

SCRIPTURE REFERENCE

"If any of you lacks wisdom, let him ask of God, who gives to all liberally and without reproach, and it will be given to him." (James 1:5)

This verse reminds you that God is ready to guide you in making wise decisions and will help you navigate uncertainty.

CLOSING THOUGHT

Believing that indecision is safe keeps you in a state of inaction and anxiety. By making decisions and embracing the learning process, you can take control of your future and unlock new opportunities. What decision have you been putting off, and how can you commit to making it today? Remember, taking action, even imperfectly, is far better than staying stuck in indecision.

Problem 84: Motivating Choices Through Fear, Not Hope

How fear-driven decisions limit your potential.

Do you often make decisions based on fear of failure or negative consequences, rather than hope for success? Many people allow fear to drive their choices, believing that avoiding failure is more important than pursuing opportunities for growth. This mindset often leads to missed opportunities, stagnation, and unnecessary stress. The problem isn't fear—it's letting it dictate your choices.

SUBCONSCIOUS INFLUENCES

Take Tom, who stays in a job he dislikes because he fears the uncertainty of switching careers. His *beliefs* that safety is more important than risk stem from past experiences where taking a leap led to setbacks. Past *memories* of making mistakes or facing criticism reinforce a *bias* that staying where he is safer than trying something new.

Tom's *fear* of failure holds him back, while his *assumptions* that change will lead to worse outcomes keep him stuck in a cycle of inaction. Motivated by a desire to avoid pain, he *expects* that fear will protect him from failure, but it only limits his growth. These subconscious patterns prevent Tom from pursuing new, fulfilling opportunities.

ROOT CAUSE

The root of this problem lies in misunderstanding fear as a protector, rather than something that should be managed. While fear can provide caution in dangerous situations, when used as the primary motivator, it leads to missed opportunities and keeps you from achieving your true potential. Making choices based on hope and possibility opens up new paths and growth.

YOUR SOLUTION

1. **Recognize Fear's Influence:** Acknowledge when fear is driving your decisions and ask yourself if hope and possibility could be a better motivator.
2. **Reframe Your Mindset:** Shift your focus from avoiding failure to pursuing opportunities for growth and success.
3. **Take Calculated Risks:** While fear may be present, take small, manageable steps toward change to build confidence and reduce anxiety.
4. **Visualize Success:** Focus on the positive outcomes that could come from making a brave choice, rather than dwelling on what could go wrong.
5. **Celebrate Growth:** Even small successes in moving past fear will help reinforce the habit of making hope-driven decisions.

SCRIPTURE REFERENCE

"For the Spirit God gave us does not make us timid, but gives us power, love, and self-discipline." (2 Timothy 1:7)
This verse reminds you that fear is not from God, and that you have the strength to make empowered, hope-driven choices.

CLOSING THOUGHT

Motivating choices through fear limits your ability to grow and pursue opportunities. By choosing to focus on hope and possibility, you open yourself up to greater success and fulfillment. What decision in your life has been driven by fear, and how can you reframe it today to move forward with hope? Remember, hope is a far greater motivator than fear, and it leads to much more lasting success.

Problem 85: Assuming First Instincts Are Always Correct

How trusting first reactions leads to missed opportunities.

Do you often trust your first instinct in decision-making, assuming it's always the best course of action? Many people rely on gut feelings or initial reactions, believing that their first impulse is the most authentic and accurate. However, this can lead to rushed decisions, misunderstandings, and regret. The problem isn't your instincts—it's assuming they're always right without deeper reflection.

SUBCONSCIOUS INFLUENCES

Take Michelle, who quickly decides to avoid a challenging project at work because her first instinct is to say "no." Her *beliefs* that avoiding discomfort is always the best choice stem from past experiences where stepping out of her comfort zone led to difficulty. Past *memories* of failed attempts at new challenges reinforce a *bias* toward playing it safe.

Michelle's *fear* of failure drives her to act impulsively, while her *assumptions* that her first instinct will protect her from failure prevent her from considering alternative solutions. Motivated by a desire to avoid discomfort, she *expects* that her initial reaction is always the right one, but this mindset keeps her from growing. These subconscious patterns prevent Michelle from making thoughtful, considered decisions.

ROOT CAUSE

The root of this problem lies in overvaluing instinct and disregarding critical thinking. While instincts can offer useful guidance, they are often based on emotional responses or past experiences, not objective analysis. Relying solely on first instincts limits your ability to make informed decisions that align with your goals.

YOUR SOLUTION

1. **Pause and Reflect:** Instead of acting immediately on your first instinct, take a moment to think about the potential consequences and alternatives.
2. **Evaluate the Situation:** Ask yourself whether your initial reaction is based on fear, assumptions, or a clear understanding of the situation.
3. **Seek Multiple Perspectives:** Before making a decision, consult with others to gain different viewpoints and insights.
4. **Trust in Logic and Intuition Together:** Use your gut feelings as one factor, but combine them with logical analysis and thoughtful reflection.
5. **Learn from Experience:** Reflect on times when your first instinct led to mistakes, and use those lessons to guide future decisions.

SCRIPTURE REFERENCE

"Plans fail for lack of counsel, but with many advisers they succeed." (Proverbs 15:22)

This verse encourages seeking wisdom from others and not relying solely on your own understanding when making decisions.

CLOSING THOUGHT

Assuming that first instincts are always correct can limit your ability to make well-rounded decisions. By taking time to reflect, consider other perspectives, and combine your instincts with logical thought, you can make choices that align with your true potential. What recent decision did you rush into based on instinct, and how can you approach it with greater reflection next time? Remember, the best decisions often come from a balance of instinct and thoughtful consideration.

ADDICTION OR OVERINDULGENCE PROBLEMS

Problem 86: Believing Escapism Solves Problems

How avoiding problems through distractions leads to deeper issues.

Do you turn to distractions or escapism when faced with challenges, believing that avoiding problems will make them go away? Many people cope with stress, anxiety, or difficult emotions by seeking temporary relief, whether through entertainment, substances, or other distractions. While these may provide short-term comfort, they only delay the inevitable need to address the underlying issues. The problem isn't the desire for relief—it's using escapism as a long-term solution.

SUBCONSCIOUS INFLUENCES

Consider Jason, who turns to binge-watching TV shows after a stressful day at work instead of dealing with the source of his frustration. His *beliefs* that distractions help him "reset" come from past experiences where temporary relief helped him manage stress. Past *memories* of feeling overwhelmed and escaping into entertainment reinforce a *bias* that distractions are the best way to cope.

Jason's *fear* of confronting difficult emotions or situations makes him reach for temporary solutions, while his *assumptions* that dealing with problems will be too hard prevent him from facing them directly. Motivated by a desire for immediate comfort, he *expects* that distractions will ease his pain, but over time, they only increase his anxiety and stress. These subconscious patterns keep him from resolving the root causes of his struggles.

175

ROOT CAUSE

The root of this problem lies in misunderstanding escapism as a solution to emotional or mental distress. While it may provide a temporary reprieve, it prevents you from addressing the actual issues, which only grow more intense with avoidance. Real growth and peace come from facing challenges head-on and taking active steps to resolve them.

YOUR SOLUTION

1. **Face Your Emotions:** Acknowledge your feelings and identify the source of your distress before seeking relief.
2. **Take Action:** Instead of avoiding the problem, take small, manageable steps to address it directly.
3. **Limit Distractions:** Use distractions as a short-term break but avoid them becoming a permanent coping mechanism.
4. **Seek Healthy Outlets:** Find activities that promote relaxation and healing, such as exercise, meditation, or creative hobbies, that allow you to process your emotions.
5. **Practice Mindfulness:** Be present with your challenges, recognizing that facing them is the only way to truly resolve them.

SCRIPTURE REFERENCE

"Cast all your anxiety on him because he cares for you." (1 Peter 5:7)
This verse encourages you to release your worries to God, rather than seeking to escape them, knowing that He will provide the support and strength you need.

CLOSING THOUGHT

Believing that escapism solves problems only delays healing and growth. By facing your challenges with courage and taking active steps to resolve them, you can find true peace and growth. What problem have you been avoiding, and how can you begin addressing it today? Remember, true peace comes from confronting your difficulties, not escaping them.

Problem 87: Associating Comfort With Overconsumption

How seeking comfort through excess leads to dissatisfaction.

Do you turn to overindulgence in food, shopping, or other pleasures as a way to feel better when you're stressed or uncomfortable? Many people associate comfort with consumption, believing that more of something will provide relief or satisfaction. However, overconsumption often leads to negative consequences like guilt, poor health, or financial strain, and it doesn't provide lasting fulfillment. The problem isn't enjoying comforts—it's using excess as a way to numb or avoid deeper issues.

SUBCONSCIOUS INFLUENCES

Consider Lily, who often finds herself overeating or making impulse purchases when she feels stressed at work. Her **beliefs** that comfort can be found in consumption stem from childhood experiences where food or material goods were used to soothe difficult emotions. Past **memories** of feeling better after indulging in excess reinforce a **bias** that indulgence brings relief.

Lily's **fear** of confronting uncomfortable emotions leads her to seek quick comfort, while her **assumptions** that more is better prevent her from recognizing the emotional triggers behind her behavior. Motivated by a desire to avoid discomfort, she **expects** that consuming more will fix the problem, but it only creates temporary satisfaction and long-term dissatisfaction. These subconscious patterns keep Lily from addressing the root causes of her stress and discomfort.

ROOT CAUSE

The root of this problem lies in misunderstanding comfort as a result of excess. True comfort and fulfillment come from addressing emotional needs in healthy, sustainable ways, not from overconsumption. Using food, shopping, or other excesses to numb feelings only perpetuates a cycle of dissatisfaction and temporary relief.

YOUR SOLUTION

1. **Identify the Root Cause:** Recognize when you're using overconsumption to mask deeper emotional issues and address those issues directly.
2. **Practice Mindful Consumption:** Be intentional about what you consume, and recognize when you're indulging out of habit or emotional need.
3. **Find Healthy Comforts:** Seek out healthy alternatives that bring comfort, such as exercise, reading, or spending time with loved ones.
4. **Set Boundaries:** Limit your access to indulgences and find ways to practice self-control when you feel tempted.
5. **Cultivate Emotional Awareness:** Pay attention to your emotional triggers and work on managing them in healthier ways.

SCRIPTURE REFERENCE

"Do not eat the bread of a man who is stingy; do not desire his delicacies." (Proverbs 23:6)
This verse reminds you that excess and indulgence are not the keys to fulfillment and should be approached with caution.

CLOSING THOUGHT

Associating comfort with overconsumption only provides temporary relief and leads to long-term dissatisfaction. By addressing the root causes of your discomfort and seeking healthier alternatives for comfort, you can find lasting peace and fulfillment. What comfort have you been seeking through overindulgence, and how can you begin to address your emotional needs today? Remember, true comfort comes from within, not from excess.

Problem 88: Fearing Limits Will Stifle Freedom

How avoiding boundaries restricts your growth.

Do you resist setting limits or boundaries because you fear they will restrict your freedom or opportunities? Many people believe that having no boundaries allows them to live more freely, but in reality, a lack of boundaries often leads to burnout, confusion, and a sense of being overwhelmed. The problem isn't having limits—it's fearing them as a barrier to freedom.

SUBCONSCIOUS INFLUENCES

Consider Alex, who constantly overcommits to projects and obligations, believing that saying "no" will limit his potential. His *beliefs* that freedom means doing everything stem from past experiences where he was praised for being adaptable and available. Past *memories* of times when limits were seen as restrictive reinforce a *bias* that boundaries are obstacles.

Alex's *fear* of missing out or disappointing others keeps him from establishing clear limits, while his *assumptions* that boundaries will limit his opportunities prevent him from recognizing their importance. Motivated by a desire to stay available and open to everything, he *expects* that flexibility equals freedom, but this often leads to exhaustion and dissatisfaction. These subconscious patterns keep Alex from realizing that boundaries are essential for maintaining balance and achieving long-term success.

ROOT CAUSE

The root of this problem lies in misunderstanding the role of boundaries in achieving true freedom. While boundaries may initially seem limiting, they are actually tools for creating space, clarity, and energy to focus on what truly matters. Without

179

boundaries, life becomes chaotic, and freedom becomes a fleeting illusion.

YOUR SOLUTION

1. **Recognize the Importance of Boundaries:** Understand that boundaries are not limitations but tools that protect your time, energy, and focus.
2. **Start Small:** Begin by setting small, manageable boundaries in areas where you feel overwhelmed, such as time management or personal space.
3. **Communicate Clearly:** Be open with others about your boundaries and assert them respectfully to create mutual understanding.
4. **Prioritize What Matters:** Focus on what aligns with your values and goals, and set boundaries that support those priorities.
5. **Embrace Freedom Through Limits:** Recognize that having boundaries actually allows you to pursue your goals with greater focus and energy.

SCRIPTURE REFERENCE

"Better a little with righteousness than much gain with injustice." (Proverbs 16:8)
This verse highlights the importance of setting boundaries to protect your peace and maintain integrity, even if it means having less.

CLOSING THOUGHT

Fearing limits as barriers to freedom only leads to burnout and disillusionment. By setting boundaries, you can create the space needed for true freedom and growth. What area in your life needs clearer boundaries, and how can you begin to implement them today? Remember, true freedom comes when you know what you can say "yes" and "no" to.

Problem 89: Motivating Habits Through Emotional Triggers

How letting emotions control your actions sabotages long-term success.

Do you find yourself acting based on your emotional state, such as overeating when stressed or procrastinating when you feel anxious? Many people develop habits that are triggered by their emotions, believing that indulging in these habits will provide immediate relief. However, these emotional triggers often lead to unhealthy behaviors and setbacks. The problem isn't the emotions—it's letting them dictate your habits.

SUBCONSCIOUS INFLUENCES

Consider Sarah, who tends to eat junk food when she feels stressed at work. Her ***beliefs*** that comfort food will make her feel better stem from past experiences when eating provided temporary relief. Past ***memories*** of being rewarded with food as a child reinforce a ***bias*** toward using food for emotional regulation.

Sarah's ***fear*** of facing stress without a coping mechanism pushes her to indulge, while her ***assumptions*** that stress will only increase without a quick fix prevent her from seeking healthier solutions. Motivated by the desire for comfort, she ***expects*** that eating will soothe her, but it only leads to regret and negative health effects. These subconscious patterns prevent Sarah from creating healthier coping strategies that lead to long-term success.

ROOT CAUSE

The root of this problem lies in using habits to manage emotions rather than addressing the emotions directly. Emotional triggers often lead to habits that provide temporary relief but don't address the underlying issue, and over time, these patterns sabotage personal growth and well-being.

YOUR SOLUTION

1. **Recognize Your Triggers:** Identify the emotional states that lead to unhealthy habits and understand why they occur.
2. **Pause and Reflect:** Before acting on an emotional impulse, take a moment to check in with yourself and assess the situation.
3. **Develop Healthier Coping Mechanisms:** Replace unhealthy habits with healthier alternatives, such as exercise, journaling, or talking to someone you trust.
4. **Practice Emotional Awareness:** Build emotional resilience by acknowledging and processing your feelings rather than reacting to them impulsively.
5. **Focus on Long-Term Goals:** Shift your focus from immediate relief to the long-term benefits of making healthier choices.

SCRIPTURE REFERENCE

"Do not be misled: 'Bad company corrupts good character.'" (1 Corinthians 15:33)
This verse reminds you that the habits you form—whether influenced by emotions or external pressures—shape your character and actions over time.

CLOSING THOUGHT

Motivating habits through emotional triggers keeps you stuck in a cycle of temporary relief and long-term regret. By addressing your emotions directly and building healthier habits, you can create lasting change. What emotional trigger has been controlling your habits, and how can you choose a healthier response today? Remember, true change comes when you stop letting emotions dictate your actions.

Problem 90: Allowing Past Dependence to Justify Current Behavior

How relying on past habits keeps you from breaking free of negative patterns.

Do you continue relying on old coping mechanisms or behaviors because they once worked for you, even though they no longer serve you? Many people justify their current habits by the comfort of past success or familiarity, even if those behaviors are no longer healthy or effective. This mindset keeps you stuck in negative patterns and prevents you from evolving. The problem isn't your past—it's letting it dictate your present and future.

SUBCONSCIOUS INFLUENCES

Take Brian, who continues to use unhealthy food choices as a way to cope with stress, even though he knows it harms his health. His **beliefs** that comfort foods once provided emotional relief lead him to continue turning to them during stressful situations. Past **memories** of when overeating temporarily alleviated pain reinforce a **bias** toward using the same coping mechanism, even when it no longer works.

Brian's **fear** of facing stress without a familiar coping mechanism keeps him stuck in this habit, while his **assumptions** that these old behaviors are still valid stop him from exploring healthier alternatives. Motivated by the comfort of past reliance, he **expects** that what worked in the past should still work today, even though the consequences are negative. These subconscious patterns prevent him from breaking free of the cycle of dependence.

ROOT CAUSE

The root of this problem lies in relying on past behavior as a crutch, rather than acknowledging that your current circumstances require a new approach. While past habits may have been necessary at one point, holding onto them out of familiarity or fear prevents personal growth and change.

YOUR SOLUTION

1. **Acknowledge the Need for Change:** Understand that past behaviors may have been effective at one time, but they no longer serve you in your current situation.
2. **Challenge Old Beliefs:** Reflect on why you still rely on outdated coping mechanisms and consider healthier alternatives.
3. **Start Small:** Make gradual changes to break free from old habits and introduce healthier practices that align with your current goals.
4. **Seek Support:** Surround yourself with people who can encourage and help you break free from old patterns.
5. **Reframe Success:** Recognize that success now requires growth and adaptation, and that holding onto past behaviors may hinder your progress.

SCRIPTURE REFERENCE

"Forget the former things; do not dwell on the past. See, I am doing a new thing!" (Isaiah 43:18-19)
This verse encourages you to let go of the past and embrace the new opportunities and growth that lie ahead.

CLOSING THOUGHT

Allowing past dependence to justify current behavior prevents you from breaking free of negative patterns and limits your potential for growth. By letting go of outdated habits and embracing healthier alternatives, you can create lasting change. What old habit are you still relying on, and how can you start to break free from it today? Remember, personal growth requires moving forward, not clinging to what no longer serves you.

SOCIAL MEDIA AND TECNOLOGY PROBLEMS

Problem 91: Associating Validation With Likes and Follows

How seeking external validation through social media keeps you from true self-worth.

Do you find yourself relying on social media likes, comments, and follows to feel good about yourself? Many people tie their self-esteem to the validation they receive online, believing that the number of likes or followers they have reflects their value. This mindset leads to insecurity, comparison, and the constant need for external approval. The problem isn't seeking connection—it's letting social media define your worth.

SUBCONSCIOUS INFLUENCES

Take Julia, who feels anxious if she doesn't receive enough likes on a recent post. Her *beliefs* that validation from others through social media is a measure of her value come from a culture that prioritizes online recognition. Past *memories* of receiving praise or attention from social media boost her *bias* that likes and follows equate to self-worth.

Julia's *fear* of rejection drives her to check her notifications constantly, while her *assumptions* that online approval defines her status prevent her from building internal validation. Motivated by the desire for external praise, she *expects* that more likes will bring happiness, but it only leads to more insecurity. These subconscious patterns prevent Julia from developing healthy self-esteem and a genuine sense of worth.

ROOT CAUSE

The root of this problem lies in misunderstanding self-worth as something external rather than intrinsic. Relying on social media for validation traps you in a cycle of comparison and external approval, which prevents you from developing true, unshakable self-esteem. True value comes from within, not from the number of likes or followers you have.

YOUR SOLUTION

1. **Shift Your Focus:** Recognize that your value is not determined by external validation, but by your actions, character, and values.
2. **Limit Social Media Consumption:** Take breaks from social media to refocus on what truly matters, and avoid seeking approval through likes and comments.
3. **Cultivate Internal Validation:** Build your self-esteem by affirming your worth from within, through self-love and personal growth.
4. **Celebrate Your Own Achievements:** Focus on what makes you proud of yourself, independent of others' opinions or recognition.
5. **Engage in Meaningful Connections:** Foster real-life relationships and connections that provide authentic support and validation.

SCRIPTURE REFERENCE

"For am I now seeking the approval of man, or of God? Or am I trying to please man? If I were still trying to please man, I would not be a servant of Christ." (Galatians 1:10)
This verse reminds you that true validation comes from God, not from the approval of others.

CLOSING THOUGHT

Associating validation with likes and follows keeps you trapped in a cycle of external approval and insecurity. By focusing on internal validation and strengthening your self-worth, you can find peace and fulfillment regardless of online feedback. How can you begin to seek validation from within instead of from social media today? Remember, your true value is not determined by others' opinions—it's rooted in who you are, not how many people notice you.

Problem 92: Fearing Disconnection From Online Presence

How relying on online connection for fulfillment weakens real relationships.

Do you worry that disconnecting from social media or reducing your online presence will cause you to miss out or fall behind? Many people fear losing their online connections, believing that their worth and relationships are tied to their digital presence. This mindset can create anxiety, loneliness, and unhealthy attachment to online personas. The problem isn't using social media—it's relying on it as your primary source of connection and validation.

SUBCONSCIOUS INFLUENCES

Consider Sarah, who checks her social media accounts multiple times a day, worried that if she doesn't stay active, she will be forgotten or disconnected. Her *beliefs* that online engagement is essential for maintaining relationships stem from the constant influx of digital interactions that reinforce her sense of connection. Past *memories* of times when social media was a platform for validation create a *bias* that her online presence defines her relationships.

Sarah's *fear* of missing out on important updates or being left behind keeps her attached to her devices, while her *assumptions* that online relationships are as valuable as face-to-face ones prevent her from nurturing real-world connections. Motivated by a desire for constant engagement, she *expects* that digital interaction will fill her emotional needs, but it often leaves her feeling drained and disconnected. These subconscious patterns prevent Sarah from fostering deeper, more meaningful relationships outside of the online world.

ROOT CAUSE

The root of this problem lies in misunderstanding the nature of connection. While social media can be a valuable tool for staying in touch, it cannot replace the depth, authenticity, and fulfillment that come from in-person relationships. Relying on online connections for emotional satisfaction prevents you from fully engaging with the world around you.

YOUR SOLUTION

1. **Set Boundaries for Social Media:** Limit your time online to avoid becoming dependent on it for fulfillment, and schedule regular breaks.
2. **Focus on Real-World Connections:** Invest time and energy into building relationships outside of social media, prioritizing face-to-face or meaningful virtual conversations.
3. **Engage with Intention:** Use social media intentionally, focusing on connection and support rather than validation and comparison.
4. **Create Offline Rituals:** Develop habits that don't rely on your phone, such as spending time outdoors, reading, or engaging in hobbies that bring you joy without digital distractions.
5. **Reflect on Real Relationships:** Regularly evaluate the quality of your offline relationships and make efforts to nurture them.

SCRIPTURE REFERENCE

"For where two or three gather in my name, there am I with them." (Matthew 18:20)
This verse highlights the value of in-person connections and the deeper sense of connection that comes from genuine, real-life relationships.

CLOSING THOUGHT

Fearing disconnection from your online presence keeps you from experiencing the richness of real-world relationships. By prioritizing offline connections and setting healthy boundaries with social media, you can find more authentic fulfillment and emotional support. What can you do today to invest in a real-world connection? Remember, true connection comes from being present in the moment, not from being constantly plugged in.

Problem 93: Believing Digital Connection Replaces Real Bonds

How relying on online interactions weakens deeper connections.

Do you believe that your online connections are as meaningful as in-person relationships? Many people rely heavily on social media and digital platforms for socializing, thinking that online interactions provide the same depth as face-to-face conversations. This mindset can lead to superficial relationships and feelings of loneliness. The problem isn't using technology—it's allowing it to replace authentic, in-person bonds.

SUBCONSCIOUS INFLUENCES

Consider Tom, who feels satisfied with the number of friends he has on social media, believing that digital interactions are just as fulfilling as meeting people in real life. His *beliefs* that online communication is equivalent to real-world connection come from the convenience and instant gratification of digital platforms. Past *memories* of feeling connected through likes, comments, and messages reinforce a *bias* that online relationships are just as valuable.

Tom's *fear* of vulnerability in face-to-face interactions makes him rely on the safety of digital connections, while his *assumptions* that online friends are just as supportive and meaningful prevent him from investing time in in-person relationships. Motivated by a desire to feel connected without facing the complexities of real-life interaction, he *expects* that digital relationships can fulfill his emotional needs, but they often leave him feeling disconnected. These subconscious patterns prevent Tom from deepening his real-world connections.

ROOT CAUSE

The root of this problem lies in misunderstanding the nature of authentic connection. While digital platforms can facilitate communication, they cannot replicate the depth, empathy, and

189

emotional fulfillment that come from genuine, in-person relationships. Relying on online connections for emotional support keeps you from building meaningful bonds in the real world.

YOUR SOLUTION

1. **Invest in Real Relationships:** Make an effort to engage with people in person, prioritizing face-to-face conversations and quality time together.
2. **Limit Online Interactions:** Set boundaries around your digital communication to ensure it doesn't replace real-world connection.
3. **Be Present:** Practice active listening and emotional availability in your in-person interactions, focusing on the depth of the connection rather than the frequency of contact.
4. **Seek Vulnerability:** Step outside your comfort zone and allow yourself to be vulnerable in real-life relationships, which fosters deeper emotional connections.
5. **Evaluate Your Social Circle:** Reflect on your relationships and make sure you're investing in those that offer true support and understanding, not just digital validation.

SCRIPTURE REFERENCE

"Better is one day in your courts than a thousand elsewhere." (Psalm 84:10)
This verse reminds you of the irreplaceable value of being present with others in meaningful, real-world connections.

CLOSING THOUGHT

Believing that digital connection can replace real bonds limits your ability to form deep, authentic relationships. By prioritizing in-person interactions and setting healthy boundaries with technology, you can build stronger connections that provide true emotional fulfillment. What steps can you take today to strengthen your real-world relationships? Remember, the deepest connections are those made face-to-face, not through screens.

Problem 94: Motivating Actions Through Fear of Missing Out (FOMO)

How fear of missing out leads to impulsive decisions and burnout.

Do you find yourself making decisions based on the fear of missing out on opportunities, events, or experiences? Many people feel pressured to act or participate in something simply because they worry they will be left behind or not included. This fear-driven mindset can lead to impulsive decisions, overcommitment, and exhaustion. The problem isn't the desire to experience life—it's letting FOMO dictate your choices.

SUBCONSCIOUS INFLUENCES

Consider Sarah, who attends social events and makes purchases based on the fear that if she doesn't act quickly, she will miss out on something important. Her *beliefs* that every opportunity must be seized stem from past experiences where missing out led to feelings of regret or exclusion. Past *memories* of feeling left behind or overlooked in group settings reinforce a *bias* that staying active and involved at all times is necessary for belonging.

Sarah's *fear* of being left out motivates her to constantly say "yes" to things, while her *assumptions* that she will miss out on important experiences prevent her from carefully evaluating what truly aligns with her values and goals. Motivated by a desire to be included, she *expects* that constant engagement will lead to fulfillment, but it often leaves her feeling drained and unfulfilled. These subconscious patterns prevent Sarah from making decisions that are aligned with her long-term well-being.

ROOT CAUSE

The root of this problem lies in misunderstanding the concept of opportunity. While it's natural to want to seize opportunities, acting out of fear of missing out leads to overextension and burnout. True fulfillment comes from making intentional, thoughtful choices that align with your goals, not from trying to be everywhere and do everything.

> **YOUR SOLUTION**
>
> 1. **Evaluate Opportunities:** Take time to reflect on whether an opportunity truly aligns with your values and long-term goals before committing.
> 2. **Set Boundaries:** Learn to say "no" to things that don't serve you, even if they seem like great opportunities in the moment.
> 3. **Practice Mindful Decision-Making:** Slow down and assess the impact of your decisions on your time, energy, and emotional health.
> 4. **Focus on Quality, Not Quantity:** Instead of spreading yourself thin by saying yes to everything, focus on fewer, more meaningful experiences that align with your personal values.
> 5. **Embrace Presence:** Let go of the fear of missing out by being fully present in the moment, focusing on what you are currently doing rather than what you could be doing.

SCRIPTURE REFERENCE

"Do not wear yourself out to get rich; do not trust your own cleverness." (Proverbs 23:4)
This verse reminds you that seeking to do everything or gain everything out of fear or greed leads to exhaustion and misaligned priorities.

CLOSING THOUGHT

Motivating actions through FOMO prevents you from making intentional, balanced decisions. By slowing down and prioritizing what truly matters, you can find peace and avoid burnout. What decision have you made recently out of fear of missing out, and how can you refocus your attention on what is truly important? Remember, it's better to miss out on a few things and stay true to your values than to be overwhelmed by constantly trying to do it all.

PURPOSE AND PASSION PROBLEMS

Problem 95: Allowing Technology to Dictate Your Time

How losing control of your digital habits affects your productivity and well-being.

Do you find yourself constantly distracted by your phone or other digital devices, letting technology dictate how you spend your time? Many people struggle with balancing their digital lives with their real-world responsibilities. Social media, notifications, and constant access to information can easily consume your attention, leaving you feeling overwhelmed and unproductive. The problem isn't technology—it's letting it control your time and priorities.

SUBCONSCIOUS INFLUENCES

Take Ethan, who spends hours scrolling through social media, even when he has pressing tasks or personal goals to address. His *beliefs* that staying connected at all times is necessary stem from societal expectations to be always reachable or up-to-date. Past *memories* of feeling left out or disconnected when he wasn't immediately available reinforce a *bias* that constant digital engagement is essential.

Ethan's *fear* of missing out on the latest updates keeps him checking his phone constantly, while his *assumptions* that he must be always "on" prevent him from recognizing the toll it takes on his focus and productivity. Motivated by the need to stay informed or entertained, he *expects* that multitasking with technology will enhance his life, but it often leaves him feeling scattered and unfulfilled. These subconscious patterns keep Ethan from controlling his time and setting healthy boundaries with technology.

ROOT CAUSE

The root of this problem lies in misunderstanding the role technology should play in your life. While technology is a powerful tool for communication and information, letting it control your time leads to distraction, anxiety, and a lack of focus on what truly matters. True productivity and well-being come from using technology intentionally, not being consumed by it.

YOUR SOLUTION

1. **Set Boundaries for Screen Time:** Limit your time on digital devices by setting specific time blocks for social media or entertainment.
2. **Prioritize Tasks:** Identify your most important tasks and set dedicated time to work on them without digital distractions.
3. **Turn Off Notifications:** Disable non-essential notifications to reduce interruptions and regain control of your focus.
4. **Practice Digital Detox:** Take regular breaks from all digital devices, especially before bed, to recharge and reconnect with the present moment.
5. **Use Technology with Intention:** Be mindful of how you engage with technology, using it purposefully to support your goals, not as a source of distraction.

SCRIPTURE REFERENCE

"Be still, and know that I am God." (Psalm 46:10)
This verse reminds you to quiet the noise of technology and the world around you, allowing space for reflection and connection with what truly matters.

CLOSING THOUGHT

Allowing technology to dictate your time drains your focus, productivity, and emotional well-being. By setting boundaries and using technology intentionally, you can reclaim your time and energy for more meaningful pursuits. What technology-related habit has been consuming your time, and how can you take control of it today? Remember, technology should serve you, not the other way around.

Problem 96: Believing Purpose Is Predefined and Fixed

How expecting your purpose to be revealed in a moment of clarity keeps you from pursuing it.

Do you believe that your life's purpose is something that should be immediately obvious or handed to you in a moment of clarity? Many people assume that purpose is something you either discover instantly or are born with, leading to frustration and inaction when they don't experience that moment. The problem isn't seeking purpose—it's misunderstanding that purpose is often discovered through intentional actions, growth, and reflection.

SUBCONSCIOUS INFLUENCES

Consider Lisa, who feels disillusioned because she believes her purpose should be obvious, like a sign she's waiting for. Her *beliefs* that purpose is fixed come from the expectation that everyone else around her seems to have clear direction. Past *memories* of others confidently pursuing careers or goals create a *bias* that she's "missing" something.

Lisa's *fear* of being lost or directionless drives her to search for an instant revelation, while her *assumptions* that purpose should feel predetermined prevent her from experimenting with different paths. Motivated by a desire for certainty, she *expects* purpose to manifest effortlessly, but she's left frustrated when it doesn't happen that way. These subconscious patterns prevent Lisa from embracing the journey of self-discovery and growth that leads to fulfilling purpose.

ROOT CAUSE

The root of this problem lies in misunderstanding purpose as a singular, fixed point that must be discovered. In reality, purpose is something that is often shaped by experiences, decisions, and the

195

journey of personal growth. It evolves over time and is often discovered as you take action and reflect on your passions and values.

YOUR SOLUTION

1. **Reframe Purpose:** Understand that purpose is not a one-time discovery but a process of growth, learning, and action.
2. **Experiment and Explore:** Try new things, take on different roles, and reflect on what excites you to learn more about your purpose.
3. **Embrace Flexibility:** Recognize that your purpose may evolve over time and that's okay; be open to change and growth.
4. **Focus on Values:** Align your actions with what you value most and trust that your purpose will emerge naturally as you do.
5. **Take Action:** Purpose is often discovered through action. Start moving in a direction, and you may find clarity as you go.

SCRIPTURE REFERENCE

"**For I know the plans I have for you, declares the Lord, plans for welfare and not for evil, to give you a future and a hope.**" (Jeremiah 29:11)
This verse reassures you that God has a plan for you, and while you may not know every detail, trust that your purpose is part of a larger, unfolding journey.

CLOSING THOUGHT

Believing that purpose is predefined and fixed limits your ability to grow and explore. By embracing the idea that purpose is discovered through action and reflection, you open yourself up to new possibilities and growth. What action can you take today to start exploring your purpose? Remember, purpose is a journey, not a destination, and it unfolds as you engage with life and reflect on your passions.

Problem 97: Fearing Passion Won't Be Profitable

How doubting the financial viability of your passions keeps you from pursuing them.

Do you hold back from pursuing your passions because you fear they won't lead to financial success or security? Many people are afraid that doing what they love won't result in a stable income, so they settle for work that doesn't excite them. This mindset prevents them from fully embracing their passions and using them to create a meaningful and profitable life. The problem isn't your passion—it's the fear that it won't be financially viable.

SUBCONSCIOUS INFLUENCES

Take Ryan, who loves photography but avoids turning it into a career because he fears it won't be profitable. His *beliefs* that passion-driven work doesn't pay stem from seeing others struggle to monetize their interests. Past *memories* of hearing about financially unstable careers reinforce a *bias* that pursuing a passion will lead to financial insecurity.

Ryan's *fear* of failure and uncertainty holds him back from taking the leap, while his *assumptions* that passion must be financially lucrative right away prevent him from seeing how it can evolve into a profitable venture over time. Motivated by a desire for financial stability, he *expects* that a traditional career path is safer, but this limits his potential for fulfillment and growth. These subconscious patterns prevent Ryan from taking the necessary steps to build his passion into something successful.

ROOT CAUSE

The root of this problem lies in misunderstanding the relationship between passion and profit. While some passions take time to become financially successful, many people have turned their passions into lucrative businesses or careers. Fear of failure prevents you from taking the necessary steps to test the viability of your passion and learn how to monetize it.

YOUR SOLUTION

1. **Reframe Profitability:** Understand that passion doesn't have to be immediately profitable—it can evolve into a financially sustainable career with time and effort.
2. **Start Small:** Begin by pursuing your passion part-time or on the side, allowing it to grow gradually without the pressure of needing instant financial success.
3. **Research and Learn:** Invest time in learning how others have turned similar passions into profitable ventures. Seek guidance from mentors who have successfully monetized their passions.
4. **Take Calculated Risks:** Step outside your comfort zone and explore ways to monetize your passion, taking calculated risks that align with your values and goals.
5. **Embrace the Journey:** Recognize that building a profitable passion takes time, perseverance, and learning from setbacks along the way.

SCRIPTURE REFERENCE

"Commit your work to the Lord, and your plans will be established." (Proverbs 16:3)
This verse reminds you that when you commit your passions and efforts to God, He will guide your plans and help them come to fruition.

CLOSING THOUGHT

Fearing that your passion won't be profitable keeps you from pursuing what could bring you fulfillment and success. By reframing your view of profitability and taking practical steps to explore how to monetize your passion, you can create a life that aligns with both your passions and your financial goals. What passion have you been avoiding because of fear, and how can you begin to explore its potential today? Remember, pursuing your passion can lead to fulfillment and prosperity—if you're willing to take the first step.

Problem 98: Assuming Failure Signals the Wrong Path

How viewing failure as a sign to quit prevents growth and success.

Do you see failure as a sign that you're on the wrong path, making you hesitant to try again or pivot when things don't go as planned? Many people view failure as a definitive answer that they are headed in the wrong direction, causing them to give up too early. The problem isn't failing—it's assuming that failure means you should quit rather than learn and adapt.

SUBCONSCIOUS INFLUENCES

Consider Jessica, who started her own business but gave up after the first few setbacks, convinced that failure meant she was not cut out for entrepreneurship. Her *beliefs* that failure equals permanent defeat come from past experiences where failure was met with disappointment or punishment. Past *memories* of hearing "you can't succeed if you fail" reinforced a *bias* that failure signals the wrong path.

Jessica's *fear* of facing further rejection or inadequacy keeps her from trying again, while her *assumptions* that failure is a reflection of her abilities prevent her from seeing the lessons in her setbacks. Motivated by a desire for success without struggle, she *expects* that failure means giving up, rather than using it as a learning tool. These subconscious patterns prevent Jessica from developing resilience and long-term success.

ROOT CAUSE

The root of this problem lies in misunderstanding the role of failure in the process of success. Failure is often a natural part of learning and growth, not an indication that you should abandon your goals. When you view failure as a final verdict rather than a stepping stone, you miss valuable opportunities for improvement and perseverance.

YOUR SOLUTION

1. **Reframe Failure:** Understand that failure is not a reflection of your worth but a natural part of the learning process.
2. **Learn from Setbacks:** Instead of quitting, reflect on what went wrong, identify areas for improvement, and try again.
3. **Embrace a Growth Mindset:** Focus on continuous improvement, knowing that success often comes after multiple failures.
4. **Celebrate Effort Over Outcome:** Recognize that trying and learning are successes in themselves, regardless of the immediate result.
5. **Build Resilience:** See failure as a test of perseverance. The more you fail and try again, the more resilient you become, and the closer you get to your goals.

SCRIPTURE REFERENCE

"We can rejoice, too, when we run into problems and trials, for we know that they help us develop endurance. And endurance develops strength of character, and character strengthens our confident hope of salvation." (Romans 5:3-4) This verse reminds you that setbacks and failures can build strength, perseverance, and character, leading to greater success in the end.

CLOSING THOUGHT

Assuming failure signals the wrong path prevents you from learning and growing. By embracing failure as part of the journey and using it to fuel your persistence, you open the door to true success. What failure have you been avoiding or afraid of, and how can you use it as a lesson today? Remember, failure is not the end— it's the beginning of the next step toward success.

Problem 99: Associating Success With Others' Approval

How letting others define your success keeps you from living authentically.

Do you measure your success by how others perceive you or what they expect from you? Many people tie their sense of achievement to external validation, believing that their worth is determined by others' approval or recognition. This mindset can prevent you from living authentically and pursuing your own goals. The problem isn't seeking feedback—it's allowing others' opinions to define your success.

SUBCONSCIOUS INFLUENCES

Consider Mark, who constantly seeks approval from his colleagues and friends to feel successful. His *beliefs* that success is about meeting others' expectations stem from growing up in an environment where external validation was highly valued. Past *memories* of receiving praise for meeting societal standards reinforce a *bias* that success is measured by others' approval.

Mark's *fear* of rejection drives him to constantly seek external validation, while his *assumptions* that he must conform to others' expectations prevent him from pursuing what truly matters to him. Motivated by the need for acceptance, he *expects* that meeting others' standards will lead to fulfillment, but it only leaves him feeling disconnected from his true desires. These subconscious patterns keep Mark from defining success on his own terms.

ROOT CAUSE

The root of this problem lies in misunderstanding success as something external, based on the approval of others. When you allow others to define what success looks like for you, you lose sight of your own values, passions, and authentic goals. True success is about living in alignment with your purpose and values, not seeking external validation.

YOUR SOLUTION

1. **Define Your Own Success:** Reflect on what success means to you, based on your values and passions, not others' expectations.
2. **Let Go of External Validation:** Learn to trust your own judgment and find fulfillment in your own progress, rather than waiting for others' approval.
3. **Surround Yourself with Supportive People:** Build relationships with people who encourage you to pursue your authentic goals, not just conform to societal norms.
4. **Focus on Growth:** Shift your focus from external recognition to personal growth and achieving goals that are meaningful to you.
5. **Celebrate Your Own Achievements:** Recognize and celebrate your accomplishments, even if they go unnoticed by others.

SCRIPTURE REFERENCE

"Am I now trying to win the approval of human beings, or of God? Or am I trying to please people? If I were still trying to please people, I would not be a servant of Christ." (Galatians 1:10)
This verse reminds you that true success comes from living according to God's will, not seeking approval from others.

CLOSING THOUGHT

Associating success with others' approval prevents you from living authentically and finding true fulfillment. By defining success on your own terms and focusing on your own growth, you can create a life that reflects your values and purpose. What areas of your life are you still seeking approval in, and how can you begin to define success for yourself today? Remember, true success is living in alignment with who you truly are, not conforming to others' expectations

Problem 100: Expecting Purpose to Appear Without Effort

How waiting for purpose to manifest without action keeps you stuck.

Do you expect your life's purpose to suddenly appear to you without any effort or intentionality? Many people wait for a clear moment of revelation, thinking that their purpose will unfold effortlessly. This mindset leads to frustration and inaction because purpose often requires proactive exploration, effort, and growth. The problem isn't expecting purpose—it's expecting it to manifest without taking the necessary steps to uncover it.

SUBCONSCIOUS INFLUENCES

Take Emily, who believes that she will discover her life's purpose one day through a moment of clarity. Her *beliefs* that purpose should be handed to her in a single, defining moment stem from the expectation that others have had "eureka" moments about their purpose. Past *memories* of seeing people confidently pursue careers or passions lead to a *bias* that purpose is something to be found instantly.

Emily's *fear* of taking the wrong path makes her hesitate to explore different avenues, while her *assumptions* that purpose will appear without effort prevent her from taking action to actively discover it. Motivated by the desire for certainty, she *expects* that purpose will come easily, but it remains elusive because she's not doing the necessary work. These subconscious patterns prevent Emily from embracing the journey of self-discovery.

ROOT CAUSE

The root of this problem lies in misunderstanding the nature of purpose. While purpose can be discovered through inspiration or reflection, it often requires active exploration, learning, and growth. Waiting for purpose to appear without taking any steps or making decisions only leads to stagnation.

YOUR SOLUTION

1. **Take Action:** Understand that purpose is often discovered through action, not in waiting for the perfect moment.
2. **Experiment and Explore:** Try different activities, careers, or volunteer opportunities to discover what resonates with your values.
3. **Commit to Growth:** Embrace continuous learning, knowing that the path to purpose often includes trial and error.
4. **Trust the Process:** Let go of the expectation that purpose will come easily. Trust that the journey itself is a critical part of discovering your true calling.
5. **Reflect Regularly:** Set aside time for self-reflection, journaling, or meditating to explore your deeper passions and desires.

SCRIPTURE REFERENCE

"Trust in the Lord with all your heart and lean not on your own understanding; in all your ways submit to him, and he will make your paths straight." (Proverbs 3:5-6)
This verse reminds you that trusting in God's guidance, while taking active steps forward, will lead you toward your purpose.

CLOSING THOUGHT

Expecting purpose to appear without effort keeps you from taking the necessary steps toward self-discovery and fulfillment. By taking action, exploring different paths, and trusting the process, you can uncover your true purpose and live a life aligned with your values. What steps can you take today to begin uncovering your purpose? Remember, purpose is found through action, not passive waiting.

CULTURAL INFLUECNES PROBLMES

Problem 101: Assuming Tradition Always Equals Truth

How unquestioned traditions limit growth and understanding.

Do you follow traditions simply because they've always been done that way? Many people uphold traditions without questioning whether they still align with their values. This mindset can hinder personal growth and understanding. The issue isn't tradition—it's assuming tradition is always true without critically examining its relevance or impact.

SUBCONSCIOUS INFLUENCES

Clara follows family traditions without questioning their alignment with her beliefs. Her *beliefs* that tradition must be respected stem from an environment where customs were sacred. *Memories* of praise for upholding tradition reinforce a *bias* that tradition equals truth.

Her *fear* of disappointing family prevents her from considering alternative perspectives. *Assumptions* that tradition is inherently right stop her from questioning its relevance to her life today. Motivated by a desire to fit in, Clara's subconscious patterns prevent her from forging her own path.

ROOT CAUSE

Equating tradition with truth without assessing its value limits progress. Understanding that not all traditions are beneficial is key to growth.

1. **Evaluate Traditions:** Reflect on the traditions in your life and assess whether they still align with your personal values and goals.
2. **Question with Curiosity:** Don't be afraid to ask "why" or challenge traditions that no longer serve you.
3. **Create New Traditions:** Embrace the freedom to establish new practices that reflect your current beliefs and aspirations.
4. **Respect Growth:** Understand that growth sometimes requires change, and change can still honor the essence of tradition while adapting it to your present needs.
5. **Prioritize Authenticity:** Choose the traditions and practices that reflect your true self, not just those you've inherited or been taught.

SCRIPTURE REFERENCE

"Do not be conformed to the pattern of this world, but be transformed by the renewing of your mind. Then you will be able to test and approve what God's will is—his good, pleasing and perfect will." (Romans 12:2)

This verse reminds you that growth and transformation come from thinking critically and being open to change, rather than blindly following traditions.

CLOSING THOUGHT

Assuming that tradition always equals truth prevents you from questioning outdated norms and finding your true path. By evaluating and adapting traditions to serve your personal growth, you can create a life that is authentic and aligned with your current values. What tradition in your life might need to be re-examined, and how can you begin to create a new path today? Remember, truth isn't static—it evolves with your understanding and growth.

Bonus Problem 102: Believing Cultural Norms Define Identity

How blindly following culture limits self-discovery.

Do you let societal expectations define who you are? Many people follow cultural norms without questioning whether they still align with their true selves. This mindset can prevent you from growing into the person you were meant to be. What if the real problem isn't culture itself, but your unexamined acceptance of its standards?

SUBCONSCIOUS INFLUENCES

Consider Maria, who grew up in a culture that emphasized the importance of family and social status. Her beliefs that she must meet certain cultural expectations shaped her choices, from career to personal relationships. Maria's memories of being praised for following the "right" cultural path reinforced her bias that success and happiness come from conforming to cultural norms.

Maria's fear of disappointing her family stops her from exploring career options outside her culture's prescribed path. Her assumptions that cultural norms are universally correct and necessary prevent her from seeing alternative ways to live authentically. Motivated by a desire to fit in and avoid judgment, she expects fulfillment through societal approval, yet feels unfulfilled, unable to align her true self with these external expectations. These subconscious patterns keep Maria from discovering her own identity and purpose.

ROOT CAUSE

The root of this problem lies in the belief that culture dictates your identity. While cultural traditions and expectations can offer comfort and belonging, blindly following them without self-reflection can prevent you from exploring and embracing your true self.

YOUR SOLUTION

1. **Challenge Cultural Beliefs:** Reflect on which cultural expectations align with your true values.
2. **Explore Your True Identity:** Discover who you are outside the cultural norms you've inherited.
3. **Embrace Individuality:** Give yourself permission to choose your own path, even if it diverges from cultural expectations.
4. **Respect Your Heritage:** Honor your culture, but recognize that your identity is yours to define.
5. **Live Authentically:** Prioritize your authentic self over conforming to societal standards.

SCRIPTURE REFERENCE

"You have let go of the commands of God and are holding on to human traditions." (Mark 7:8)

This verse highlights how clinging to traditions without questioning their relevance can prevent personal growth and true alignment with one's purpose. It speaks to the danger of allowing external influences to dictate our identity, rather than evaluating whether those traditions serve us or align with our values.

CLOSING THOUGHT

Believing cultural norms define your identity limits your ability to explore who you truly are. By questioning these norms and embracing your individuality, you can live a life that aligns with your true self and values. What aspects of your culture do you need to re-evaluate, and how can you begin to embrace your authentic identity today?

Bonus Problem 103: Allowing Biases to Shape Worldview

How unconscious biases limit your understanding and relationships.

Do you ever find yourself making judgments about others based on assumptions or stereotypes? Unconscious biases influence how we see the world and interact with people, often without us realizing it. These biases can limit our ability to connect with others, understand different perspectives, and grow as individuals. The real problem isn't the bias itself—it's allowing it to shape your worldview and interactions without challenging it.

SUBCONSCIOUS INFLUENCES

Consider John, who instinctively feels uncomfortable around people from different cultural backgrounds. His *biases* were formed early in life by the environment he grew up in, where certain groups were stereotyped. These biases were reinforced by *memories* of hearing negative comments about these groups, shaping his perceptions.

John's *fears* of unfamiliarity and change prevent him from seeking diverse perspectives. His *assumptions* that people from other backgrounds will act in a certain way keep him from fully engaging with them. Motivated by the desire to avoid discomfort, John *expects* that interacting with people from different cultures will be difficult, which stops him from forming meaningful relationships. These subconscious influences keep him from experiencing personal growth and understanding.

ROOT CAUSE

The root of this problem lies in unchallenged biases that limit your perspective. These biases, though often unconscious, shape how you see and relate to the world, preventing deeper connections and growth.

YOUR SOLUTION

1. **Acknowledge Your Biases**: Reflect on how biases may be shaping your thoughts and behaviors.
2. **Challenge Assumptions**: Question preconceived notions about others and their experiences.
3. **Seek Diverse Perspectives**: Engage with people from different backgrounds to broaden your understanding.
4. **Practice Empathy**: Approach others with curiosity and empathy, embracing their uniqueness.
5. **Reframe Judgments**: Replace biased thoughts with open-minded perspectives that celebrate diversity.

SCRIPTURE REFERENCE

"Do not judge by appearances, but judge with right judgment." (John 7:24)
This verse encourages you to look beyond surface-level assumptions and approach others with fairness and understanding, breaking free from biases that limit true connection.

CLOSING THOUGHT

Allowing biases to shape your worldview prevents growth and meaningful relationships. By challenging your biases and embracing diverse perspectives, you can develop a more inclusive, open mindset. What biases in your life are limiting your understanding, and how can you begin to expand your worldview today?

Bonus Problem 104: Avoiding Triggers Instead of Processing Them

How avoiding emotional triggers hinders healing.

Do you avoid situations or topics that trigger emotional reactions? Many people try to shield themselves from pain by avoiding triggers, but this can delay true healing. While avoiding triggers may provide temporary relief, it prevents you from addressing the underlying emotions that need to be processed. The real problem isn't the trigger—it's avoiding it rather than confronting it and allowing yourself to heal.

SUBCONSCIOUS INFLUENCES

Consider Emma, who avoids discussions about her past trauma because they make her feel overwhelmed. Her *memories* of painful experiences make her reluctant to revisit them. These *memories* reinforce her *fear* of experiencing the same emotional pain again. Emma's *assumptions* that confronting her past will only bring more hurt keep her from addressing the root cause of her emotional struggles. She *expects* that avoiding the trigger will help her maintain control, but in doing so, she remains stuck in her unresolved pain.

ROOT CAUSE

The root of this problem lies in the belief that avoiding emotional triggers will protect you. While avoidance may seem like an easy way to cope, it prevents healing and personal growth by keeping painful emotions buried.

> **YOUR SOLUTION**
>
> 1. **Identify Triggers**: Recognize what causes emotional reactions and why.
> 2. **Face the Pain**: Confront emotional triggers in a safe and controlled way.
> 3. **Process Emotions**: Allow yourself to feel the emotions, rather than suppress them.
> 4. **Seek Support**: Engage with a trusted person or therapist to help you process difficult emotions.
> 5. **Reframe Triggers**: Reframe your perspective on triggers as opportunities for healing and growth.

SCRIPTURE REFERENCE

"He heals the brokenhearted and binds up their wounds."
(Psalm 147:3)
This verse reminds you that healing comes when you confront your wounds and allow God to restore you.

CLOSING THOUGHT

Avoiding emotional triggers may seem like a way to protect yourself, but it only delays true healing. By processing your emotions and facing what triggers you, you can move past the pain and experience the healing you deserve. What emotional triggers do you need to face, and how can you begin the healing process today?

About the Author

Allen Brown is a lifelong minister and successful entrepreneur whose journey with Christ began on Easter morning in 1998, leading to a profound commitment to ministry in 1999. With over twenty-five years of experience in Christian ministry, Allen has dedicated his life to uplifting believers, spreading the gospel, and equipping others with practical tools to grow spiritually and succeed in life.

Married to his devoted wife, Melissa, for 27 years, Allen is the proud father of four young adult sons. Together, the Brown family has built a strong foundation centered on faith, family, and business. Allen's entrepreneurial journey began early in life—his first structured business at age 18 led to remarkable success, including generating millions of dollars in revenue and creating employment opportunities for many.

Currently, Allen focuses on his passion for writing and empowering others through *Build Our Kingdom Publishing*, a company dedicated to producing Christian-based books that inspire believers to align with God's purpose. As a published author of multiple transformative works, Allen shares wisdom drawn from his faith journey and entrepreneurial experiences to help individuals embrace their God-given potential.

In addition to his publishing work, Allen is an active public speaker and community leader. He delivers motivational and faith-based messages designed to encourage growth, resilience, and spiritual alignment. Through his outreach efforts, Allen continues to inspire communities, emphasizing the power of biblical principles to transform lives.

For more information about his books, speaking engagements, and ministry, visit **www.allenbrownministries.com**.

When not working on new projects, Allen enjoys spending quality time with Melissa and their sons. Together, they exemplify the values of love, perseverance, and service, reflecting Allen's unwavering commitment to glorifying the Lord and empowering believers to thrive in every aspect of life.

About Build Our Kingdom Publishing

BUILD OUR KINGDOM PUBLISHING
——— BUILD OUR KINGDOM.CCM ———

WE ARE A CHRISTIAN BOOK PUBLISHER WITH THE FOCUS ON
PUBLISHING NON-FICTION LITERATURE TO EDIFY AND BUILD THE
KINGDOM OF GOD.
OUR VISION IS TO SEE PEOPLE COME TO JESUS CHRIST
AS A RESULT OF THE TITLES WE RELEASE.

FOR MORE BOOKS BY ALLEN BROWN
VISIT BUILDOURKINGDOM.COM

Million Dollar Seed

How My Last $17,600
Grew to Millions God's Way

"Million Dollar Seed" tells the extraordinary journey of faith, obedience, and divine intervention that transformed the author's final $17,600 into a thriving financial and spiritual breakthrough. This inspiring narrative goes beyond material success, exploring the profound impact of trusting God's guidance in the face of uncertainty.

The author shares candid reflections on challenges that tested and strengthened his faith. Paralleling his experiences with biblical figures like Abraham, the story highlights the timeless principles of faith and obedience in unlocking God's blessings.

Structured around three pivotal phases—life before Christ, awakening faith, and a deep trust in God—the book provides a roadmap for spiritual growth and personal transformation. More than a financial success story, "Million Dollar Seed" reveals the deeper wealth found in peace, joy, and alignment with God's purpose.

A source of motivation and practical wisdom, this book invites readers to trust in God's plan, persevere through challenges, and embrace the limitless possibilities of divine guidance.

I Will Teach You How to Hear God's Voice

In a world filled with distractions, hearing God's voice can feel elusive. Yet, the opportunity to connect with the Divine is closer than you think.

In *I Will Teach You How to Hear God's Voice,* Allen Brown draws from his own profound experiences to illuminate the path to divine communication. Through compelling personal stories and biblical wisdom, Allen unveils the life-changing power of hearing and following God's voice in every area—family, business, finances, and ministry.

This guidebook dismantles doubts and affirms that God yearns to communicate with you, guiding you toward your unique purpose. Packed with practical exercises and spiritual insights, it equips readers to cultivate sensitivity to God's whispers, interpret His silence, and deepen trust and faith.

More than a book, this is an invitation to discover a relationship with God that transforms your life. Let His voice be your guiding light.

The Christian Entrepreneur's Compass Volume 1

33 Biblical Strategies for Growing Your Business

"The Christian Entrepreneur's Compass Volume 1" by Pastor Allen Brown offers 33 powerful strategies to help entrepreneurs align their businesses with biblical principles. Drawing from timeless lessons in Scripture, Pastor Brown highlights stories of figures like Isaac, Jacob, and Joseph, transforming their experiences into actionable insights for modern business challenges.

This guide provides a unique blend of faith and practicality, encouraging readers to balance profit with purpose while building ethical, God-centered businesses. Each chapter delivers wisdom and tools to navigate today's marketplace with integrity and spiritual growth at the forefront.

Perfect for entrepreneurs, leaders, and professionals seeking to integrate their faith into their work, this book serves as a roadmap to lasting success. Whether starting a new venture or enhancing an existing one, "The Christian Entrepreneur's Compass Volume 1" inspires readers to achieve business goals while fulfilling their divine purpose.

Escape the Rat Race: God's Way

ESCAPE THE RAT RACE
GOD'S WAY

DISCOVER BIBLICAL SECRETS THAT CAN
UNLOCK YOUR PATH TO FINANCIAL FREEDOM

Pastor Allen Brown

"Escape the Rat Race: God's Way" reveals a divine path to financial freedom and spiritual abundance. This transformative guide combines biblical wisdom with practical financial insights, offering seven foundational principles—Faith, Obedience, Sacrifice, Wisdom, Resourcefulness, Gratitude, and Generosity—that lead to true prosperity as ordained by God.

More than a financial manual, this book is a roadmap to a life of purpose, fulfillment, and impact. Each chapter weaves practical advice with spiritual truths, making it accessible to anyone seeking a deeper understanding of wealth and success. It challenges conventional ideas of prosperity and invites readers to embrace spiritual richness alongside material abundance.

Whether trapped in the monotony of daily life or searching for greater meaning, "Escape the Rat Race: God's Way" inspires a shift in priorities. Experience wealth that transforms not just your bank account but your heart and spirit. Start your journey to lasting joy, peace, and divine prosperity today.

101 Relationship Problems That Steal Your Joy

101 Relationship Problems That Steal Your Joy offers a powerful guide to overcoming the challenges that hinder joy in your relationships. Whether you're single or in a relationship, this book addresses the problems that create emotional distance, dissatisfaction, and frustration. You'll uncover key issues, such as miscommunication, unrealistic expectations, unhealthy patterns, and the deep-rooted beliefs that prevent connection and happiness.

Each problem is explored through real-life examples, subconscious influences, and practical solutions you can start applying immediately. This book empowers you to break free from destructive cycles, build stronger connections, and foster deeper, more fulfilling relationships.

The complete guide provides valuable insights for both individuals and couples, offering actionable steps to reclaim happiness and create the love life you deserve. Don't let unresolved problems stand between you and your fulfillment. Start your journey toward a better, more joyful relationship today!

www.ingramcontent.com/pod-product-compliance
Lightning Source LLC
Chambersburg PA
CBHW071713140626
46557CB00011B/76